Creative Teachers: Who Wants Them?

Creative Teachers: Who Wants Them?

Robert O. Hahn

Professor of Secondary Education
California State University Los Angeles

John Wiley & Sons

New York   London   Sydney   Toronto

Library of Congress Cataloging in Publication Data

Hahn, Robert O.
Creative teachers: who wants them?

   1. High school teaching. 2. Creative thinking
(Education). I. Title.

LB1607.H16   373.1′1′02   73-6592
ISBN 0-471-33905-9

Printed in the United States of America

10 9 8 7 6 5 4 3 2 1

To
    My
        Wife, Genevieve

To
    My
        Sons, Christopher P.
           and
         Peter Q.

Preface

In American public education small voices and meager samplings, as well as mass media and political lobbies, may rightfully bear witness to its processes and products. But one man's voice raised against any present practice in the institutional life of a democracy must at last be justified by whether or not it is utilized merely for self or for society, "the other self." As a teacher of teachers, my voice and viewpoint are focused herein on a small, possibly central phase of education—teacher creativity in secondary schools. My purpose is to persuade into action all parties involved in education (administrators, teachers, students) to expose, examine, and exorcise any spirits preventing the release of full human potential in the teaching profession. Many teachers, some students, and most administrators may claim that this presentation is a biased, bitter, and sometimes unjust mixture of fact and feeling. Others may see situations, people, and activities very much like their own experiences and say, "Yes, I was there, too!" And still others may wonder what my voice is shouting about.

To those creative teachers who are still facing the barrage; to those who faced and ran; to those who are just about to face that first class, this book is dedicated.

Los Angeles, California   *Robert O. Hahn*

Acknowledgements

If the creative process has any meaning to me, I recognize that the words in this book have probably all been thought before. But the painstaking process of putting them down on paper in this particular form needed assistance, and in this attempt I have been most fortunate in having had the services of the keen eye, sharp ear, and constant questioning and insistence on clarity of Mary Miasnik, my typist and editor.

The names of some of the creative teacher-souls who have touched mine need to be recorded: Miss Hackett of the eighth grade (we were never allowed to know their first names); Angela Boboy and Anna Alberico at the high school; Earl O. Butcher at the college; Sawyer Falk at the university; Donald MacNassor and James Finn at the graduate school; Wendell Cannon and Marian Wagstaff at the schools of education. All of these CT's were not only creators in their own right, but believed in the creativity of each of their students and ignited the spark in this particular one.

Contents

Part III *Every-CT: Gauged, Gouged, But Still Grooving*

Creative Teachers: Who Wants Them?

Overview

Creative High School Teachers: Wanted or Not?

I was a CT—a Creative Teacher. I wanted to teach kids, to spend time with and energy for them. I was certain that I could bring excitement into any classroom. I did. We created together, my students and I, and my students were enthusiastic.

Then the noninstructional, red-tape curtain fell! Administrators (any professional yet nonteaching member of the school staff who serves the teachers and students) became enemies. If I wanted to take my students on a field trip, I had to fast-talk the superintendent in charge of finance. When I attempted to introduce controversial topics such as economic inequality or racial discord or sex (I never even whispered the word) into the curriculum, the subject-matter supervisor discouraged me. If I requested permission to assign a novel that depicted modern teenage life realistically, the department chairman said, "Forget it!"

My education professors had assured me that the top on-site administrator, the principal of the high school, would assist me in maintaining a creative instructional program; but each time I walked into his outer office seeking counsel, either the door to his sanctum was closed or his formidable secretary barred the way.

I am no longer the creative teacher I once was, and I blame that paragon of secondary school administration—the principal. Because I sought his advice and aid on behalf of the students he assigned to me,

1

I felt the greatest allegiance toward him. Why had he let me down?

Although my very personal point of view will be presented here, I speak for other teachers who have confided to me that they faced the same frustrations I did. I can hear their voices now:

> *I was a social studies teacher, but when I mentioned in class that a third political party, the Socialist, was also listed on the ballot in the coming election, I was not retained.*

> *I taught biology and took seriously the school district's mandate to instruct my students about sex; within the week I was asked to leave the district.*

> *I argued with the principal about the retention of the word* pregnant *in a play script. That was the last opportunity I had to direct a class play.*

> *I was an English teacher who used the Gettysburg Address, as it would have been corrected by an English teacher, as an example of the intricacies of style. After being scolded by the superintendent, I left the classroom to become a school librarian.*

> *I encouraged my history class to investigate the viciousness of rumor by developing with them a "clinic" involving the entire student body. I didn't get a permanent appointment.*

Most administrators I know were classroom teachers once, communicating with and relating to their colleagues in warm, helpful relationships. But something happens to the inter-relationships between principal and teachers after the former has accepted his new responsibility.

At the risk of arguing the administrator's case, I can recognize certain forces that might cause him to forget so soon that he also experienced the same expectations and frustrations as his staff does now. Among the personal imperatives, maybe administrators never were creative teachers. They might not have found satisfaction from interacting with students and actively sought to escape that relationship. Possibly their

2

goal was not to stand in front of a group and assist the learning process but to sit behind a desk and mind the other activities of the store. To them, perhaps teaching was only a means, not an end in itself. Then, too, their motives might have been solely economic since as administrators they would receive higher salaries than as classroom teachers.

There could also be talk-oriented pressures. For instance, administrators appear to relate more closely to the upper echelons—supervisors, counselors, superintendents—than to the corps of teachers or mass of students in school. Also, they seem to become more concerned with material factors (finances, building supervision, schedules) rather than with the instructional aspects of the school program. Again, since an administrator is no omnipotent one-man band, he sets up a number of subprincipalships—designated as department chairman, coordinators, and the like—to implement other administrative obligations (equipment, books, extra-duty assignments). Still another force impinges on him from the community the school serves—fund drives, booster club demands, essay and speech contests. Difficult to handle one by one, all these pressures in confluence represent overwhelming power which seems to stifle rather than enkindle innovative, relevant teaching stratagems initiated by the teaching staff. The administrator may say publicly that the "schools are being run for the kids" but too often spends his energies on the "things" of the school situation. Deliberately or unwittingly, he begins more and more to associate his teachers with "things," the means of education, rather than with "kids," the purpose of education.

And the teacher in the classroom, that personality I label a CT (creative teacher): what happens to him in this system? Trying to function with any degree of reality under these dynamics, he loses direct touch with his administrator. He, too, begins to see himself as more of a "thing" than a personality and becomes less creative in all his relationships. His separation from the administration may be partly responsible for the fact, often stated blatantly by teenagers, that most activities in the high school classroom are "boring and irrelevant to life." As he operates in the "thing" syndrome, he is frequently unwilling to change many of the accepted (but not tested) debilitating routines of the classroom. He may attempt once or twice to arrange an exciting field trip for his students; he may also take heart and investigate a controversial issue or two, perhaps inviting provocative and articulate "outside" guests to participate. But upon discovering that he is no more than a statistic in the downtown (district) office, that he is not really being supported and often is thwarted by another supposedly creative force in his principal, he soon realizes that his own creativity is losing potency.

3

Our CT's dilemma is obvious. If he is forced to choose among his allegiances, teacher-to-principal rather than teacher-to-student, he frequently cuts off sources within his students, such as atypical perceptions and different experiences, which might assist him in developing a more creative climate in his classroom. If, on the other hand, he chooses to relate more to his students, he will very likely attain CT status and at the same time perhaps lose touch completely with his administrator. Thus, he tries to relate to his principal and fails; he has little access to those persons in the hierarchy of the "downtown" arm of the administration who choose and assign the principal—personnel directors, assistant superintendents, the "Big Boss," or members of the school board; his students and their parents are not empowered to assist either. Complicating this process further is the fact that no human being, expending physical and psychological effort to maintain a creative learning situation for five periods a day of at least forty minutes each with approximately thirty-five students in each class, can relate equitably and fully to two such demanding responsibilities.

The third "R" in the reading-'riting–red-tape curriculum is too much for him to face, is too great a frustration. With his creativity shattered or maimed, the CT may seek solutions to his problems or assuage his anxieties in professional organizations. But few teachers have the strength, courage, or even the time to present their case to those professional organizations to which they are committed. The CT needs encouragement and assistance in functioning as an innovative leader in a classroom of adolescents. Without it he struggles on, doing the best he can to teach as creatively as possible within administratively superimposed limitations, all the while beset with unresolved tensions which imprison his own creative spirit.

As a teacher myself, involved with students first and systems second, I propose some general remedies as a partial solution to the problem of teacher-principal relationships, hoping that those persons involved in the educational establishment everywhere will give them consideration.

The total secondary school program needs re-examination, particularly that area of interaction between principal and teacher, in order that the learning process becomes the focus of both persons and that the creative energies of each are utilized fully for the best benefit of the student. To initiate such a re-examination, we would do well to direct our attention to provocative questions such as the following:

1. Can administrators be relieved of business affairs in order to function more creatively with their teachers as innovators and partici-

pants in the school program? (The principal is described in a hundred administration textbooks as the "director of learning activities.")

2. Might experimentation with the election of principals by the teachers in the individual schools be a possibility? (Such action might put the control and communication in better order and eliminate the middleman entrenched in the downtown offices.)

3. Does the differential in salaries of the principal and teacher set up a barrier between them? (The salary discrimination between elementary and secondary teachers has been erased. Why continue the discrimination between teachers and administrators?)

4. How large should the school population of a junior or senior high school be in order that personal communication among principal, teacher, and student be maintained? (Eight hundred students for junior high schools and no more than one thousand for senior high schools has been recommended.)

5. What should the class load per day and the class size for each teacher be? (For the most effective communication, one hundred students per day and four teaching periods would be more psychologically feasible.)

Other ways of freeing the creative spirit of educators might be suggested, but let the above suffice to begin the process of re-evaluation and reflection.

Somewhere the spirit of the only experiment in secondary education, the "Eight-Year Study" (1932–1940), still roams the educational corridors and may once again permeate educators' thinking, encourage them, and set free the creative spirits of administrators, teachers, and students. To this end the subsequent chapters are divided into three sections. Part I portrays intimately one lonely Odysseus and his wanderings through the administrative sea. Part II examines a series of confrontations between administrators and several creative teachers who never completed their voyages. Part III probes the dynamics of the two major forces involved and makes suggestions for a possible reconciliation which might establish the climate in which creativity may flourish. Thus the material flows: from background to drawing board, and thence with luck, to full flight.

5

Part I

One Creative Teacher—An Odyssey

How the lonely traveler, who,
By himself,
Found himself;

How those whose lives he touched,
Some,
Kept him from finding
More of himself;

And others,
CT's,
Helped him find
The most of himself.

Chapter 1

Creativity in Teaching— or What In The Hell Is It All About?

He called himself creative; he had come to that conclusion as he lived in and traveled through the various classrooms—elementary, secondary, and collegiate, hearing the word repeated by teachers and professors as well as reading about the process in the literature. At times during his preservice training he thought the entire world of education centered its activities around the creativity concept; at other times as he sat in dull, uninteresting classes, he wondered where the concept had fled to. Were the critics of education (consisting of every articulate son-of-a-bitch who could draw a breath but wouldn't set foot inside a public school classroom) justified in relegating the word *creative,* along with other educational terms, to the pedagoguese graveyard? Or did the word really contain a relevancy and reality for each student, teacher, and administrator operating in the public school environs?

His title, CT, was self-imposed at first; he hadn't analyzed what he was as much as determined what other teachers he had observed were not. Reading what the experts (not many) had written about the elusive subject of creativity (not much) had not moved him; he was impatient with words and eager for action. One of his students, evaluating him as a teacher, had written, "He's a good gardener, and one can get a good high on what he cultivates." He wanted to be shown, not talked

9

to, and thus far among his former teachers and now colleagues he had witnessed too little action. The questions multiplied: Why were there so few capital "C" creative teachers? Or were there? What had happened to the "dedication" of their student teaching days? Were there external variables in the total process that inhibited their freedom and therefore their creative efforts? Were they born or were they made?

Our hero had begun the search for his own creative spirit very early during his elementary school experience. As he sat in one classroom after another, how-I-would-do-it thoughts ran through his mind. "If I were that teacher, I would have asked this question, would not have been satisfied with that response, done this, not have done that." The public school became a place where he satisfied two demands: companionship with his peers and acceptance from adults who evinced interest in him and his creative self. Each successful response received in the classroom welded him more closely to the teaching act. His peers queried: "Would you teach me how to do this math problem?" "Have you done your English assignment? May I read it?" "Would you take part in this play we want to do for the Thanksgiving assembly?" Teachers inquired: "We'd like you to recite the Gettysburg Address at the soldier's cemetery on Memorial Day." "Would you help me correct this set of spelling papers?" His creative spirit responded to those teachers in whom he found a kindred spirit operating. To him, all the days he spent in school were fulfilled needs harnessed irrevocably with acceptance.

ACCEPTING—Was this one of the components in the total configuration of teacher creativeness? Was our hero's creativity activated because he was at first acceptable to those adults who functioned as his teachers? If the human organism manages to survive the birth trauma, if the environment of the earth accepts, then creativeness has a place to germinate. Further, each organism already functioning in the world must accept its fellow survivor in order that his own survival may be assured. Translated into pedagogical operations, this means that all persons involved in education must accept, for what each is, the other.

> I accept you, student, because you are
> As I am, a part of me and the universe.
> Whatever you are, am I, and I am you.
> Together we move through time
> To the same end.

Must the CT accept them all as they are? Is his action so different in the classroom from every other human being's activity? The lawyer: does he not too accept? The doctor: should he not if he does not? Do each of these recognize the otherness in himself? Or is the teacher unique in this?

> You, adolescent, hate me, the older one, before you.
> You cannot bring yourself to accept
> This dying mass before you when you are all
> Alive and invincible.
> "This earth will not do to me what it has
> done to him,"
> you say.
> And all at once the image before you becomes
> A mirror, and you turn away because you
> Know now that what will be standing there
> Is yourself, your own image, hated too.

Different from doctor and lawyer is his acceptance, yes. CT must accept them all at once, while medico and counselor take them on one by one—eyeball to eyeball—or do they really ever look each other in the soul of the eye?

Thirty, forty adolescents stare, dissecting him, while his gaze must be directed in forty different directions at once. Accept them all, each and every? Impossible! And yet the force which moved him into that front-of-the-classroom spot insists, demands, commands.

At first he seeks out those eyes that half-smile, to at least partially meet with his, understanding that he and they are in this together though eons apart in time. But other eyes and half-turned-up lips say, "Not me, baby; I'm not buying." Still, CT must deny that they are there—those half-smirks, those I-dare-you looks, those nothing-gazes that neither accept nor reject but just are.

Then he moves to neutral ground, the reason they are met together, now until the end—that exploration into words and meanings of a thousand subjects to discover whether there is any answer to that eternal question, WHY? Here, if he can move them to accept him as he accepts them—in trust—the journey into mysteries will probably be a joyous one.

So the CT, having built an accepting community in his classroom, accepts also the administrator, provider of the means of instruction, who in turn accepts the CT with full confidence that he will make that instruction meaningful. All accept concurrently and reciprocally. Each recognizes that without acceptance of the other's individuality and creativity his own uniqueness or even personality will wither and die.

Inherent in this assumption of acceptance as one of the criteria for

11

a creative climate is the interaction principle of the late psychiatrist and personality theorist Harry Stack Sullivan. If no person exists as a creative organism unless he relates to, negatively or positively, another such as he, then acceptance is not merely a conjecture or substantiation of the creativity concept but is essential for survival. Each of the players in the educational drama exists because of the other—functions, creatively or not, because the other *is*. The principal would be a lonely body on the steps of his building were the teachers and students never to arrive on that opening day of school. He *is* because they *are*.

When the environment has accepted him, the fount of creativity upon which the CT can draw begins to flow. Because of this activation, he also incurs a responsibility, and he has a debt to pay. CT must return some part of his own being to that environment that welcomed him into the living cyclorama. He therefore pledges himself to that second component necessary to maintain the creative atmosphere.

Our CT, having accepted the younger, more immature members of his atmosphere, now exercises the second ingredient of the formula— SHARING. He extends that reciprocal responsibility and debt to his brother-creators in the educative process.

And with the giving comes the getting. He not only shares his accumulated gifts but accepts those offerings that his students bring. For no matter how extensive the being of our CT, knowledge and experience are in reality a happening of the past while his students are a happening of the present. As he stands before or sits next to that student —encouraging, coaxing, or even at times threatening, he recognizes that his accumulations are but temporal gifts.

> You and I are only flecks
> In the universe
> Which become visible or tangible
> Only when the radiation pulses from me to you,
> Flows between us.
> If I lend you mine and you yours,
> Something appears which is more than us—
> An idea, a plan which
> Will move us on
> In our search for reality.
>
> My loan to you
> Is that of more experience in time,
> More about the old-man's-world,
> Its hopes and hazards,
> What the stage of man's work is like
> And why.

12

Your loan to the larger pattern
Which we both are making
To time on earth
Is that of energy, no thought of end,
Only beginnings;
A searching insatiable for different avenues
To life today around us.
You bring the voices of youth
To be heard,
Examined,
And moved upon.

Yes, our CT must accept and share, but he must be allowed to function in an educational climate of total sharing. In the American educational system, the responsibility for the maintenance of such an atmosphere has been assigned to the in-house administrator—the principal. For if the dynamics of sharing extend only unilaterally, e.g., from the teacher to the student and not from the administrator to the teacher, the process will be a tenuous one and the climate cloudy. Once an administrator has made a selection and appointed a teacher to a position in the classroom, he must accept and share with him.

Somehow the atmosphere set up within a school building where the first and second components of creativity are operating mystically, psychically, or magically, permeates almost every classroom and the life-space of its students. They can sense whether a sharing process is radiating and very often respond in a like manner. It is made evident to the students by the way in which teachers greet each other and their students in the hallways. If the principal drops into a teacher's classroom for a friendly chat, the tone of his voice is recognized as warm or cool and is responded to by the students. In essence the climate generated within the school is reminiscent of that which exists within a family unit in which "good mornings" are exchanged for the seven-thousandth time at the breakfast table; in which each "goodbye" is only a "see-you-later"; in which is echoed always the theme, "we're glad you're alive because only with you living are we alive."

Our CT's creativity is nurtured, broadened, and maintained for the students' benefit within certain climatic conditions that exist at the administrative level as well as at the level of classroom activities. In practice the responsibility of the administrator would be primarily exhibited in his concern for the instructional program. Is the student functioning creatively in the classroom? More, is the CT's own creativity being fostered both by the general climate of the facility and particularly by the principal's perception of his role as the director of learning activities?

13

As the CT becomes more creative in the atmosphere of acceptance and sharing, a third component of the creative process seems to arise. That student who is accepted and with whom the teacher now shares—knowledge, experience, and feelings—must now be moved to an involvement, an activity, a commitment, to that creative kernel within him which says, "Do something with me; make some impress on the environment around me, or else we do not survive or live, but merely exist." The CT has recognized all of the above in himself; and since he is self-directed, he naturally accepts the responsibility of this third component, STIMULATING.

> I have found most of
> Myself
> And in the discovery
> Cannot contain the
> Energy aroused;
> It must be shared—
> More—
> The pulsing must pass
> To you
> Or I shall not find
> The rest of me.
> The flash of thought
> Demands

First

> *Reflection* with
> You sitting on my shoulder

Then

> *Revelation*
> My brain put this on me
> But stands meaningless
> Without you.
> Your brain must
> Share the electricity
> And tell me
> To move ahead with you

Now

> *Thrust* ahead
> Force every cell to yield and
> Work, think, organize each electron
> Into units which in joining
> Will make the
> Whole of you

14

And
The whole of me.

Then

Pause
For both of us
To check
The going and the way
For a brief moment
And then
Continue
To the end.

Finally

Announce
To all around
Our joined
Failure or success.
The world will know then
That
Movements
Have been made
On its roughness
To smooth
The living of
All.

In order to develop each student's potential fully he must go beyond accepting and sharing to that point in the creative process where activity is aroused. The very fact that he stands before these adolescents now in this clearly delineated role is often sufficient to activate students to approach that same role in the society around them. A radiation, a vibration is established in that classroom that does move students into action.

Of course any activity must be implemented by those techniques already practiced and developed by the CT in his professional training and experience. The students must be made aware of his commitment not only by the aura that the CT exudes but by his actions and examples as well. No doubt student resistances are there or will arise, resistances to the CT as an adult figure to be mistrusted, as an authority figure, a representative of the "school" system; but the truly dedicated teacher, secure in his role, will ignore the resistances to him in these perceived roles, confident that these students who have come two-thirds of the way with him through the acceptance and sharing phases will also walk the rest of the way to individual commitment and action on their parts.

15

The stimulation or facilitation may come in a variety of guises—according to the basic personality of the CT himself—blustering, quiet, coaxing, threatening—but always recognizable by the students as "I accept the fact that he's really trying to help me find myself and a suitable goal for me in society."

You move me? No Way.
Not today or any day
Unless
You can find in that
Heart and soul of me
That which none but
I can see.

I shall keep it locked
Tightly
Within me
Until I sense that your
Searching
Is not only for you but for me too.

Show me by sounds and movements,
By silences
As we move toward and away from
Each other,
That you wish to awaken those
Inner-most thinkings
For me and mine,
You and yours.
Then I shall open the
Palm of my heart to you.
Not before.

A thread that runs through and brings together all three aspects of creative teaching—accepting, sharing, and stimulating—and acts as a catalyst to the total process is emotion, the affective nature. The total dynamics of the three functioning ingredients is that of human relations—administrator to teacher, teacher to student—a cyclic relationship irrevocably bound to the almost intangible and immeasurable emotional involvement.

Too often the intellectual conditioning to which our CT has been exposed becomes a substitute and an excuse for rationality without feeling. "Be objective; be distant," says the totally intellectual, committed crusader to those who would teach. He influences college students to think that intellectuality alone, the cognitive domain, might be at some time completely divorced from the emotional. Perhaps this point of view is a legacy from the era of the TEST—the Intelligence Quotient, the I-Summation, with little consideration for the E or emotional. Or it may be a holdover from the Age of Reason that has been transferred through the academic community, which for the most part has had a major role in shaping the thinking of the "teacher in the public school."

At present the over-reaction of some young people to the seeming lack of feeling within the educational structure to the point of complete irrationality has given some academicians pause; sociologists and psychologists are moving desperately, especially those involved with the educational process, to redirect the energies that might lead to a violent social revolution in the seventies, one untempered by either reason or controlled emotionality. An expression of the dichotomy evident in American society is that between those who speak of "law and order" and those who consider "law and justice," tempered with mercy, to be of paramount concern. Today's educational problems are more often rooted in gut-level emotionality than cold-blooded rationality—witness student riots, unhappy dropouts, the drugged, and the disadvantaged. And how difficult it is for those who hold that all life is reasonable and realistic to deal with those human beings whose frustrations have driven them to unreasonable acts! The old rules seem no longer to apply, and our value system is bombarded with students' cries of "irrelevant."

Creativity in teaching denies neither I nor E but demands synthesis. The creative, the imaginative is as much an emotional mechanism as an intellectual one. What the creative teacher senses most quickly is that dearth of feeling from his superiors which is the enemy of the process designed to stimulate more of the same. He also resents the arbitrary directive, the deference to rules and regulations, which often is the result of intellectual reinforcement only. So as he must be simultaneously the recipient of a monolithic stimulation, the intellectual inseparably intertwined with the emotional, he must approach his daily task of teaching with the constant awareness of the feeling as well as thinking involved.

In order to assist the CT with this difficult chore, let us hear the creative administrator say:

I have examined your proposal,
observed your interaction with the
students, listened to your plea; and
although on paper, in the classroom,
and to my ears it sounds unrealistic,

*impossible, and radical, my feelings
are tempering my rationality; it might
just work for you and your students. I
wouldn't attempt such a project. The
outcomes are not clear to me, and the
design is somewhat erratic. But I
guess that's the creative process. I
have faith—go ahead.*

What an encouraging message to that CT making the effort to probe and explore creative avenues to learning with his students even though the final outcome of such exploration might be failure! At least he and they would have traveled together in the "processing," which is the key to real learning.

Is that it? Have we just described and synthesized those inner workings of our CT? Is he really, for the purposes of communication on at least one level and for the moment in time that we share, that teacher who so stimulates his already accepted and sharing students by the originality of his thought patterns that they are encouraged to seek out that internal force which will free them to think, feel, and function in a manner which is uniquely their own?

If creativity is any or all of these—acceptance, sharing, and stimulation growing within the double-jointed womb of intellectuality and emotionality—let the process begin!

Chapter 2

A Long Beginning: A Short Ending?

In upper New York, the State (never to be confused with New York, the City) rested a small town, almost a suburb of a larger, more populated city a mile away. Something had happened to the teacher of the American history class, and a substitute was needed at once. The placement agency had said that the job might become permanent after a two-week trial. Our hero-CT accepted and entered his first classroom. Perhaps his geographical search up and down the state, in and out of administrator's offices, on busses and off trains had finally ended and his search for the creative kindred spirit was about to begin.

The textbook was one used in many such schools: written to the criteria of schools' needs and authors' competencies. As in all other classes, the excitement evoked from it depended upon the teacher's interpreting for the students. By great good fortune two seemingly unrelated events converged that week that stimulated the creative impulse of our hero.

The students were in the middle of a unit of study on the Twenties and were discussing certain reformers such as Upton Sinclair, Lincoln Steffens, and Sinclair Lewis and their influences on such disparate topics as meat packing, journalism, and morals. It was also a presidential election year. The opportunity for connecting some of the revolutionaries of the Twenties with this evolutionary event was a natural course of

19

action, or so thought the instructor. He listed the possible candidates for office on the blackboard.

Reflections.......................................

Many social science teachers would have had no compunction about letting the chalk fall into the tray after the names of the Republican and Democratic candidates had been properly inscribed. After all, they were the only men in the race who had a chance of getting elected. But wait! These youngsters were trying, with the teacher, to recapture some of the feelings as well as the facts of the Twenties, a moment of history when more than two political parties were able to marshall forces to support their candidates.

.... End Reflections

One of those former candidates, a Norman Thomas, was still an active campaigner. Our CT mused:

Should my students be made more
aware of other national interests
represented on the ballot?

In the long run, isn't the presentation
of alternatives a major responsibility
of each social studies teacher?

Do similar alternatives exist even
today for these students and their
parents?

For this particular instructor, the decision was not a difficult one. So, fatefully, the chalk continued to make its mark on the blackboard, inscribing for the first and perhaps last time in this small upstate New York schoolroom the name of the Socialist candidate for the presidency.

Another day went by, two more, and the students and teacher were getting acquainted. The students seemed interested, even involved, and our CT was striking certain responsive chords. An excitement about history was beginning to generate an atmosphere in which many of the textbook facts were coming to life.

You mean people ate that stuff until
The Jungle was written and the food
and drug laws passed?

Can we bring some of the sample

20

> *ballots into class and vote for our
> choices?*

> *How come our last history teacher
> never let us talk like this?*

The fourth day, and then a summons brought our CT to the principal's office. He expected that his search of several months for a permanent position, not easy to find in the 1930's, had ended and that a contract for at least the remainder of the semester was to be offered. But the principle of alternatives which the instructor had so proudly invoked in the history classroom was not present in the administrator's "classroom," the front office.

> *Did you write the name of a Socialist
> on the blackboard and discuss him
> with your students?*

*Yes, just as I did the Democratic and
Republican candidates for the
presidency.*

Then came the long, kind, but administratively prescribed message:

> *You realize that this is a very small
> community, populated by very
> conservative citizens.*

> *Some members of the school board
> still own and operate farms. They are
> not interested in having their
> youngsters exposed to radical
> viewpoints.*

> *Why, no one in this town would ever
> consider voting for the Socialist
> candidate. Many of our townspeople
> do not even recognize, much less
> acknowledge the name of Norman
> Thomas.*

> *A few members of this community,
> especially among the school board,
> feel that a social studies teacher
> ought not to be involved in politics.*

> *If you consider yourself a Socialist
> sympathizer, I'm afraid we have no
> place for you on this faculty.*

No alternatives. It was a short stay.

21

Reflections..............................

This was our CT's first encounter with the organized forces that opposed him. The daughter of a member of the local school board had reported the incident to her father. He, in turn, had spoken to the principal, who had relayed the message. The initial moment of truth again focused our hero's attention on his perception of creative teaching, this time out of practical necessity.

He knew and had known for many years that teaching was to be his life's profession. An excitement seized him every time he thought about a classroom filled with students. It even possessed him as he planned the activities for the next day. In fact, almost all of his reflections day by day, hour by hour, were about his students, real or imagined, and how they might or might not respond to his ideas. Of his own power to motivate, to instigate change he was confident. But the vision of the overpowering administrator through whom he had to go to gain access to a classroom confused and frightened him.

Each time he was interviewed by a principal, that confidence and drive, surging inside when he faced his students in the classroom, withered. The principal-specter arose to reject, withhold, and stultify. The adolescents who sat in front of him in the classroom somehow fed his own creativity. But in the principal's office he perceived no such encouragement or stimulation. The only image conjured up was one of a series of charts which propounded rules, rhetoric, and resistance.

He had always thought that the administrator and the teacher had a primary and mutual concern—the student. Were the worlds of the teacher and administrator actually so far apart? Was this encounter, although isolated in time, place, and personalities, a portent of an unforeseen pattern which was more realistic than he had been led to believe? Were all principals to be considered enemies, representative of forces which worked against creativity?

Throughout his search for a position in the upstate New York area, his contacts had always been with either principals or superintendents. What if men such as these were always to be his only evaluators. How could he adequately present his case, vitally proffer his qualifications before these men, make them realize that he could teach well.

His first attempt to be an authentic, creative teacher by presenting alternatives to his students had failed. And in his struggle to be creative he had found no ally, no cooperative, responsive force to encourage his innovations or even suspend judgment while he tried an imaginative, worthwhile scheme to implement learning. He had searched for that creative atmosphere in which both he and his students might flourish, where existed only the ideas and feelings of each at that all-important and all-possessing moment regardless of whatever ideas and feelings had gone before or were yet to be born. Only a crystallization of their thinking and feeling together would result in the moving ahead with confidence toward success or failure.

But in the face of such obvious lack of support, perhaps a threat that he might never be allowed to teach at all, much less teach creatively, our hero had some second thoughts. Should he move on then, searching, or end the search before it had begun?

.... **End Reflections**

Chapter 3

Ghosts Across the Boards

No one cared whether anything creative was going on in the classroom. No one ever visited it. Only the ghosts who trod the boards of the old Colonial Theater knew the truth.

Our CT's first full-time job: college students this time to work with, to inspire. The anticipation of meeting them, a group he might share knowledge and experience with, was almost more than he could bear. Open the door to that classroom! Bring them on!

But the doors never opened. In fact, they were nailed shut—and tightly. To begin with, the theater stood apart from the main campus, several blocks away from the mainstream of collegiate activity. The campus buildings rose on a knoll which was not likely, he discovered, to be stormed by a newcomer.

The community itself was an isolate, cut off by historical provincialism, by surrounding mountains, nestled in a valley which collected high humidity in summer and damp bitter winter winds. It was an island not easily invaded by change. Townspeople and college people alike refused to be disturbed by any fresh breaths of modernism, political or social. Inbred, almost incestuous, self-conscious and self-confident—a natural part of the northeastern scene.

He wondered whether any human beings were around. Few students sauntered by the theater; it was not in the path of quad traffic. He rarely saw other faculty members. He learned circuitously about the tightly knit social milieu within the college community. Once before he had witnessed such a revelation in his alma mater, which closed

24

its doors to the outside world and gamboled in its own narrow intellectuality and immorality. A more-than-loyal alumnus had written a book which spelled out the scandalous inbreeding, and a paid inmate of the college had promptly bought up all the copies.

Below the knoll and in the prison house of drama, the game of bridge was the great divider between "ins" and "outs." If one were invited to play and met the incestuous criteria, he moved into the social circle—parties and dinners and upward on the rickety ladder of promotion.

The smells of the social garbage heap on the knoll reached him through the speech and drama department activities. His superior was not only the chairman; he *was* the department, a law unto himself in his closet drama. His programs were designed as entertainment for the "ins." The students and his assistants were merely tools, puppets in the Gordon Craig manner.

The chairman's assistant, our CT's former classmate and now colleague, was not allowed to teach: nor was our hero, the instructor. In their initial interviews they had received such a promise. At no time was either in charge of an activity remotely connected with students and learning. They were forbidden even to speak to the chairman's students:

> *If you students have any questions, I'll answer them.*

was the chairman's intrusion if a student were caught chatting with either the instructor or assistant. What the boss wanted was personal slaves who were allowed to use the library, under his strictest supervision, only to check bibliographies. They suspected that the sweet librarian was a counterspy who reported verbatim in a faculty memo any conversation between her and them. Oh, they were permitted to type a few letters, were consigned to moving scenery from one storage dock to another, much as the army digs a second hole as a place to put the dirt from the first hole. To top it off, the seemingly unholy two never attended a faculty meeting, were never included in any special events sponsored by the faculty. Even the Christmas Party—no room at the inn for them. Social, nonacademic events to which they were entitled were never even mentioned.

Like a nightmare which lingered till morning, each day began with the chairman entering by the front of the theater—stomp-stomp-stomping his way down the aisle and around to the backstage area where his minions occupied a cell-like office, issued orders and reprimands and stomp-stomped his way back to his own office in the front of the theater, where he perched, eagle-eyed, waiting for signs of conspiracy

25

against him—the order not carried out to the inch, the unforgivable contact with students, the time wasted. Obviously no nesting place for creativity.

However, our CT survived disillusionment about not being allowed to teach. The periphery with its centers of creativity saved him: across the road from the castle of nightmares sat a gabled boardinghouse, forbidding until the door opened to let out the warmth and brightness of Mrs. Deiglmeyer's and her savory fare. Also, the German professor's home was a peaceful sanctuary where both the instructor and the assistant roomed. The Congregational Church had a lively, liberal minister. And there was a friend, a musician, whose every movement was creative from his fingers on the keyboard to his scratched musical notations on manuscript paper, from legs that climbed mountains to eyes that saw the movements and ears that heard and identified the songs of birds. The C in our CT survived because of long, fruitful discussions at the dining table, tailgating long into the night in Mrs. D's parlor; the German professor's concern with Schweitzer's hospital at Lambarene; the Congregational minister's stimulating sermons; and the long hikes up Camelback Mountain with his musician friend.

Comments at the boardinghouse—or rather the lack of them, the deadly silence following his announcement of status and supervisor at his first encounter with his fellow boarders, warned him that the melodrama in which he found himself was evolving into a serious black comedy.

> *Hope you finish the year. The last*
> *instructor . . . well.*

He produces good plays, but . . .

> *Doesn't say much at faculty meetings.*

His wife is a flower—by name, that is.
But watch out.

> *His students tell me that only the*
> *favorites talk to him.*

> *Well, good luck.*

From the creative atmosphere of the boardinghouse to the non-atmosphere of the playhouse. Only a step away, yet a world away as the huge front door closed behind him. No creativity, no teaching, no nothing. Hour after hour he planned excitement for the classes he had been promised, on paper. His colleague was less patient, more resentful and activist than he. Somehow the chairman, in his perhaps twisted assessment of department personnel, made a fine distinction between instructor and assistant. He strained out any invectives or cursing when he spoke to the former but included them when addressing the assistant, thus keeping his cool with one, and blowing it with the other.

I wish you would follow directions.
Why the hell can't you follow orders?
Come here a minute—please.
Get your f____ing ass over here,
____berg.

Seeing the assistant rapping with a student sent the chairman into a fury. There was literally nothing for either of them to do, yet they both had to appear occupied, and not with each other. They never conversed within the walls of the old theater unless the boss was not in the building, and even then they were never certain of his absence or presence. They wept and commiserated to each other only when wrapped in the warmth of the boardinghouse or the small white frame refuge of Herr Professor. It was a new world to the assistant, used to the urban, sophisticated, open climate of the large university.

As the winter snows piled up outside the playhouse, verbal abuse piled up inside, more and more against the assistant. Then the blow to our hero.

Said the professor:
Move out of that house!
Replied the instructor:
Why?

There's collusion between you and him.
I can't.

Move!

Twisted, pulled one way and another, the instructor sought advice from the musician, the German professor, even the minister.

From them:
Hold your ground.
He doesn't have the right.
Someone's got to break the chain.
To the chairman:
I won't.

27

Hell, hell, and more hell broke loose. He knew each morning what the stomp-stomp would bring: pound-pound-pound on the desk:

I order you to move!

Move! Move! Move!!!

And then the screaming rages would die away, only to return again the next day.

It finally happened.

You dirty conniving Jew bastard!

He grabbed him by the shoulders, spun him around, kicked him, and sent him sprawling down the stairs. Without responding by word or gesture, the assistant arose, walked out and up the path to confront the man on the knoll—men, a triumvirate, because the president of the college was on leave for the year.

Even the president wouldn't have known the names of the instructor or the assistant in the speech and drama department. The three administrators' names were a mystery to the two protagonists. Both parties were nameless to each other. The charge made by the assistant was a shock. It was corroborated by the instructor because only he and he alone knew the torture of the theater. But all the ensuing communication between the "three" and our CT was by written communique only. Never once was he interviewed or asked to testify verbally. It was as though they didn't want to admit that any other human being was involved in the mess except the assistant.

There was a hurried decision. The assistant was paid the balance of his contract and advised to leave the campus at once.

Pandora's box had been opened, and during the investigation other evidence turned up which labeled the chairman at least "sick." His paranoid tendencies were verified—evidently by other witnesses (our hero was never officially informed), and the triumvirate moved swiftly and completely. None of them wanted even a shred of the dirty linen around. Chairman and instructor were also dismissed.

Reflections ....

Blow number two. How many more he could endure and for how long he didn't know. There seemed to be no one to strike a blow FOR creativity. There was no accepting, sharing, or stimulating. He pondered:

One noncreative, paranoid professor:

Only I teach. You stay in the background.

28

Two creative teachers:

We want to teach, to help.

Three uninvolved administrators:

*Who cares who they are or where
they come from.*

*Underlings, only underlings. I am the
boss.*

We hurt, feel abused, unused.

*Don't get emotional. Keep it quiet.
Disappear.*

.... **End Reflections**

In the end two creatives had to be discarded with the uncreative—nay, the destroyer. Though two were innocent and only one guilty, the powers that were could not separate them, could not deal with each one individually and justly. The administrators' guilt at having allowed such a situation to arise and grow without having stemmed the tide several years before made them want to cut off the entire arm and leave not even the stump.

The assistant, traumatized by the experience, became a teaching dropout. His accomplice, the instructor, went on to another possibly frustrating experience. Would his creativity again be used as a weapon against him?

Chapter 4

Don't Cross Your Principals Even After You've Come to Them

The secretary said do this. The secretary said don't do that. There she was: a mere secretary who could administer a junior high school all by herself. She stimulated her own brand of creativity: accuracy, promptness, and neatness of innumerable written reports required by the administration.

Reflections.......................................

In many public secondary schools efficiency and effectiveness are rated principally on the basis of administrative trivia—ADMINIS-TRIVIA. Adhere to the budget. Tote-up that barrage of absences! Lift that baleful record of reading achievement scores!

.... **End Reflections**

The school on the hill and to the north of the city could not be called a school with a creative atmosphere but merely an institution in which creativity was condoned. You might, if you were with the "ins," the right political party of the poker-playing crowd, get special films, go on field trips, grab off a more sizable hunk of the budget. But to "arrive" from wherever you were, you had to make it with "that" secretary. The principal, whom we shall label NCP (noncreative principal), had surrendered the day-to-day operations to her. If she liked you because of something that clicked in her head, she saw to it that you traveled with the right company in the community. And she duly notified the principal that you were suitable for the classroom. She operated *in loco principalis* (LP) while he, (NCP) continued to puff contentedly on his cigar, seldom leaving the sanctuary of the teachers' room—the principal's hideaway, as the staff called it. He sat and smoked the days away, unaware of anything about anything that was going on in the classroom, least of all about what was happening to the students.

That cigar, the ritual of the cigar, was what our CT remembered most vividly ten years removed from the smoke-filled teachers' room. It was a pleasant place with light from the north and comfortable sofas. But the odor was of the principal's making. Only rarely did a teacher enter the calm; the rhythmic ascension of clouds and rings seldom faltered even during those crises that precipitated an invasion of his privacy:

*I can't find that film I ordered last
week. I need it—like last period.*

> *Oh, see LP about it.*

*That science equipment; it's been
sitting on the loading dock downtown
for a week now.*

> *The delivery men gotta have a break
> once in a while, don't they?*

*You promised two weeks ago we'd get
those reading books for my class.*

> *Oh, now CT. You don't really want to
> bug those kids with more books, do
> you?*

*How can we have a Spring Concert in
four weeks without music? You got
those football helmets in five minutes
when Coach ____ spoke to you about
them.*

> *Oh, didn't LP tell you? The Board cut
> the music budget last July. No
> concert.*

Our CT, now older and wiser but nevertheless imprisoned in the noncreative atmosphere, fell into a livable pattern, again mostly outside

31

the school community. First, he had gained insight into the secretary-principal relationship by carefully observing her behavior. Besides her eccentric measuring rod of creativity, she would bring a student up sharply if he dared to enter her domain:

> *What's Mr. ____ sending you down here for?*
>
> *Why does he want so much paper?*
>
> *You tell him to be careful with that key. He lost the last one.*

Then again, when new teachers applying for jobs came for interviews:

> *I'll see that you get to be one of the gang.*

Since LP, not NCP, appeared to be the instigating power within the school, he nurtured this true source and prospered all his days. She was a pockmarked woman at least ten years his senior. Although he was not too attractive physically, he possessed youth, vigor, and imagination. By dating and flattering her, he was able to demand and get what he needed to function creatively in his classes.

To back up his creative social acuity, he worked the other side of the street as well. It did not take him long to learn that the principal administered—the few times he did make decisions—on the basis of personal feelings. Those who did special favors for him could do much as they pleased for and with their kids. They might get their students excused from *all* their classes, for the day perhaps, for special projects—stagecraft, for example, no matter the protests of their fellow teachers. NCP's favorites were never called upon to chaperone at school dances. Those who didn't cater to his peculiarities languished. The friends of his friends were granted extra supplies when, according to LP, there were none; others went without.

Before long CT learned that the smoke-blower loved to see films of the band parading or the football team charging. Although he knew nothing of cinematography and abhorred the rah-rah of football, he marched miles up and around the town's cobblestoned streets and football field, pointing the damned infernal machine at kids and faculty and parents, letting the spool whirl away madly. The gyrating flicks, shown only in the privacy of the sanctuary, warmed the principal's heart and moved him to grant our CT special favors: in math classes, string to make geometric figures and the space in the lobby display case to exhibit them; in the science lab, rats and cages for experimentation; in dramatic productions, expensive rented costumes.

The hurts thus administered by the principal or LP to the faculty-outs went deep, and rarely could the total teaching staff muster enough support to implement policies that might enrich the students' lives. On one side were the teachers who played the favorites' game for their own benefit. On the other were the NCT's (noncreative teachers), whose creativity had been neutralized through time and frustration. The thrust and energizing were expended in personal skirmishes rather than in total devotion to the purpose of furthering the educational operation. More, envy and greed developed in greater proportions:

> *You can't borrow* my *projector.*
>
> *I got those supplies for* my *project alone. Why don't you get your own?*

Our CT, who had learned to play the game for his students' enrichment, felt pangs of guilt as he recognized his brothers' plight. He tried to make amends by being generous with his acquired materials and special activities. Sometimes he made suggestions as to how the neutralized ones might reactivate themselves.

Meanwhile, back in the classrooms, the students sat on the sidelines observing the strange phenomena and tried to figure out the moves on the upmanship chessboard, wondering all the time if this weren't really the game of life after all everywhere. If they wanted a project approved, they knew where the power structure was and didn't bother with the neutralized ones. Respect for the various teachers and their classroom wares vacillated as the pawns were checked and mated.

Reflections...

The moss-backed social structure behind the ivied walls of public secondary schools consists of the principal as leader; the vice-principals, counselors, and department heads as middle administration; and the teachers—novice or veteran, CT or NCT, as soldiers in the front-line trenches, the classroom, where the action is. Most differences among schools usually depend upon the perception of the principal in his role as leader.

The Dr. Strangelove–type principal of the north, while looking longingly at his not-too-far-distant retirement, apparently perceived his leadership role as similar to a military hierarchy. And he puffed out his days the easiest way he could. He turned over all possible operations to his exec-sec, LP, dispensed orders to his favorites, and ignored the grunts. Accept he would, if the troops came from the same geographical area. Share he might, with favorites through LP. Stimulate he could not, his vision smoke-clouded by self-imposed exile.

.... **End Reflections**

The social milieu outside the indifferent school walls also had an impact on our CT and encompassed the second aspect of the livable pattern. Although labeled a city on the map, it was a small cluster of humanity deposited on the west bank of a great river and near a larger metropolis. Older residents paid homage to each other and were the traditions of the town. Republican, conservative, it had tried to maintain its closed-ness and isolation from the mainstream of American society.

But the Depression brought in poor laborers, industrial and agrarian, who made inroads into the small culture. During the thirties this new group demanded financial support from the federal government, in opposition to the inner group, and secured two junior high schools, built with WPA funds, for their children. That complex to the north where our CT functioned represented the older, more conservative elements in the community.

The junior high school in the south was headed by a newcomer, who was able to delegate some of his authority by encouraging creativity in his teachers. He had no sanctuary and wanted none. He was all over the place all the time—halls, classrooms, fields, offices. Even his speech reflected his concern for putting first things first—people before things:

For the kids' benefit, and yours too,
we should establish a longer
homeroom period. They need your
guidance. You need the time to give it.

Also, the teachers from his school were outspoken in teacher organization meetings. He stimulated and blessed their efforts. They suggested, challenged, proposed resolutions. The teachers of the north who attended these meetings heard, and fled—to the south, to bask in the warmer creative clime and be listened to by the CP (creative principal).

Reflections ....

He had been trained, this CP, in the same batallion of administrators as the principal of the north and went into his school in the south with similar perceptions of his role as leader. Seemingly unaware of the change, however, he gradually separated the facets of papers and people. He delegated no financial or legal authority to anyone. That buck stopped at him. But in the realms of instruction and personnel, he began to move almost unconsciously into the role of facilitator. Accept he did; share he would; stimulate he had to.

He accepted each member of his staff as a professional—competent, sensitive, communicative. He shared with all of them—his time, energy, experience. And he stimulated them all. He gave the CT's in his school their heads as well as his own assistance in any form—materials, downfield blocking, encouragement. With the NCT he tried to revitalize those dormant abilities which he knew had been only momentarily stifled. And this is what principaling is all about.

.... **End Reflections**

Despite this double-barreled polarity—conservative-noncreative vs. liberal-creative—our CT established personal relationships with all the community groups and survived for three years because of his involvement in the dramatic arts.

All his life, from Sunday school recitations to roles in school plays to participation in WPA-sponsored theaters he had been active in the nonprofessional theater. His eyes, ears, even nose were alerted to any group which shared his interest. He exchanged ideas with one colleague who saw him as a prospective member of the Civic Community Theatre and gave him the signal. Our hero read it loud and clear.

What a contrast to his previous sojourn! Now the building used for play production became a haven and stimulus rather than the former horror turn-off. He acted, stage managed, directed—all the while making connections outside the school walls that enriched his own and his students' lives. He used the resources provided by influential citizens who were active in the theatrical venture.

He followed the example of two other CT's who had met the challenge of remaining creative. As a buffer against the indifferent NCP, they had moved into the community with their energies. And with revitalized spirits they returned to the school scene to stimulate their students. Long ago the more veteran of the veterans had organized a community choral group to which a goodly portion of the small-big town considered it an honor to belong. His students progressed with natural ease from school chorus into the community group to complete the cycle.

The other CT, a young band director, found solace and acceptance in his church. Soon the organ pedals rebounded to the pressure of his 250-pound frame. The remuneration from this job gave him the wherewithal to buy those records for his students. Music resounded in the hearts of the hardened citizens and moved them to supply the bonds necessary to continue the music program. So the laymen supported where the principal of the north reneged.

Our CT functioned so well in extracurricular environs that he was able to capitalize on his achievements. He moved, not into the creative southern clime, but into a more open senior high in the western section. With happy-unhappy feelings he left his junior high kids. Although he would miss the noisy, inquisitive bunch, in a few years he knew they would be with him once again, and so they were.

The freer atmosphere allowed him to implement more exciting activities. For three years he flourished, at last really able to teach. Because he had become an accepted member of the in-group, he was able to function much more creatively in his new position by establishing a sound dramatic program. He encouraged the creativity of students in the areas of composing, playwriting, acting, and scene design. He developed the tradition of the annual field trip into the gossamer world of the Broadway theater. He contributed his own and his students' talents to the already vital community theater. The cycle in drama was as complete as the one in music.

However, he was not more creative there because the principal accepted, shared, and stimulated him. Although the personality was different, the role this NCP played was the same as that of the NCP of the north. Slow in step and slower in thinking, he also had relinquished the immediate and long-range decisions to his LP.

Once there had been a place on the baccalaureate stage for the white-haired, dignified supernumerary. But internecine wars and rebellious youth had set that all aside. Now he stood nervously behind the counter that separated him from sullen faces and raucous, demanding voices.

No respect for their elders

he muttered again and again until it echoed in his brain and drove him to immobility. He turned away, seeking refuge behind closed office doors.

Let LP do it.

Reflections..

In this case NCP was turned off—completely, resigning and relinquishing authority to an underling who might or might not be with the scene. If she were with it, CT's and students are fortunate. If she were not, oppression and frustration set in, completely devastating them. So acceptance, sharing, and stimulation might be dependent not on NCP but on LP, the exec-sec.

.... **End Reflections**

This LP was a different breed of cat—higher bred she was, and she stood higher than her boss on the IQ scale. Calmer and resigned to her maidenhood, with sublimated sex on the side with the creative choral director, she was kinder and wiser, respecting the creativity of those teachers she greeted in the morning and assisted throughout the day:

I'll call downtown to see whether they can't hurry up that order.

If you want me to call and make that appointment, I'll be glad to. I know how much time you're spending on rehearsals these days. How's it going?

Don't worry about missing faculty meeting. I'll explain to NCP.

Reflections.......................................

Accept she did, so smoothly and quickly that her boss never noticed, not that he really cared. Sometimes a teacher's sartorial eccentricities made her question inwardly his competency in the classroom. But she delayed her judgments about him until she heard her service students discuss his teaching techniques enthusiastically. She then dismissed her doubts all together.

Share she did also. Often a teacher approached her desk belligerently, questioning the reasonableness of certain forms he had to fill out. Patiently she waited until his emotion had cooled, then quietly explained the purpose of the forms. At the same time she gave him hints as to how to complete them more quickly.

Stimulate she tried. With a subtle suggestion she could remind the not-too-exciting math teacher that he might be doing his students a favor by teaching them how to figure out and complete an income tax form.

.... **End Reflections**

And in this setting our CT flourished. He had made his peace with that in-group to which she, like the LP of the north, was a contributing member—dinners, parties, theater functions. He still lived in the community and could see from the third floor of the high school west the roofs of the junior high school north. He often exchanged gossip with former colleagues who still inhabited the creativity-forsaken place.

But he did not escape entirely the arm of his junior high principal of the past three years. The third factor in his nonacademic creative life style was his interest in the local teachers' organization. Because he spoke out for policies such as salary increases and more faculty participation in policy-making, he was elected president. His former principal was also a member of the group and especially vocal when the superintendent's cause needed support:

> *He says that it will be impossible,*
> *according to his budget, to find money*
> *for raises for teachers.*
>
> *There will be no teachers' advisory*
> *council while he's superintendent!*
> *And I know he means it.*

Dissatisfaction became more vociferous against mistreatment by state legislators, whom teachers depended upon for pay raises and professional advancement. A group of extremely rebellious cohorts in an upstate city had finally walked out. The teachers throughout the state actually said the word STRIKE aloud as they read the strong expressions of sympathy in professional journals. In many communities teachers' organizations demanded that their members stand or sit but be counted nevertheless.

Our CT's group was no exception. The day came for a final decision about whether or not to call a meeting to consider a sympathy walkout. He stood at the rostrum, recognizing various members during the discussion.

Two hands went up. One belonged to a member known to be in favor of calling an emergency meeting. The other belonged to his cigar-smoking former principal. The decision to recognize one before the other had to be made in a split second. There was the possibility that the principal's hand had been raised a fraction after the teacher's. He called on the teacher.

In that moment a passing parade of all the inadequacies of administrators seemed to flash before him in quick succession like the rattle of a machine gun. He would never really know what made him choose as he did. Nevertheless, the teacher spoke, and the emergency meeting was called.

The principal stalked out of the meeting.

A Pyrrhic victory followed, and the strike was stillborn. Our hero got the word that the principal had vowed to "get" him. Shortly thereafter the principal, who had always been a confidant of the superintendent, just managed to retain his position when the latter was found guilty of embezzling school funds. The district's half-adequate school system and the lack of long-term, top-level creative leadership contributed the additional impetus. Our CT was on his way west.

Reflections.......................................

Assuming that some operations of any school are for the most part a mechanical process, the head man, P (principal), should have considerable time to devote to the encouragement of creativity on the part of the teaching staff. In some schools this happens, but more often the creative teacher alone initiates any creative efforts. Perhaps this is the ideal situation—each teacher his own creator. For creative efforts to be sustained, however, there must (or ought to) be some recognition—a reward, or at least acceptance.

Some teachers can operate in an uncreative or sterile school atmosphere for a time, but without a response from some administrator their creative urge can be stifled. Other, more timid teachers can never begin to realize their innate creativity without some positive stimulation and protection from the administration, either principal or supervisor.

All principals choose their role as leader in the school. They are not forced to make this decision. If they don't play it with conscience, their followers, CT's and students, are betrayed, wither, and die.

.... **End Reflections**

Chapter 5

Joshua Fit the Battle of Desert-O

The pioneer spirit—escape, change—still exists in the teaching world, more mobile now in the twentieth century. Teachers move from city to city, city to country, go abroad on fellowships, take Peace Corps assignments, or travel on sabbaticals offered by the wealthier, more enlightened school systems.

A trip west—new worlds to conquer, or perhaps be conquered by.

Our CT had heard from others and had read in professional journals about the exciting events in the educational world of the west. The idea of a community college intrigued him; and his restlessness, brought on by professional frustration, moved him by '34 Classic Ford across the country.

Try CTA.

Someone said, and after translating the initials into California Teachers Association—Southern Section, he did. The high activity of impressive offices spelled professionalism. The reception he received gave him the feeling that here was a state so creative and professional as to be served from north to south by a teachers' organization striving to benefit teachers and maintain high standards.

Don't leave. Stay in the state. We'll find something for you.

To that date, he had not yet resigned his eastern post, but with such encouragement he dispatched that telegram that severed all bonds.

The position offered him was in a school district whose complicated initials took him three years to learn. The first glimpse of the parched buildings and broad expanse of apparent desolation made him yearn for the verdant river valley he had just turned his back on. The job didn't offer him the junior college teaching he wanted, but he accepted.

At the initial interview the creative tone he heard in the superintendent's voice dispelled any leftover doubts. He knew the creative spirit was there because the questions he was asked demanded that the answer be listened to:

*Our desert rats are just as curious
and hungry for knowledge as the city
kids. Do you think you can supply
some of the answers to their
questions?*

*I understand you're interested in an
advanced degree. What specialty do
you intend to pursue?*

*Do you plan to stay in this position,
or is it merely a stop-gap?*

The superintendent also indicated that he knew what was going on inside and outside the classrooms of his schools and was interested in maintaining that desert vitality he appreciated as unique. He not only knew about all the activities but the names of all the students involved in all of them—and their families!

*Our service clubs are interested in
sponsoring school events and getting
our kids known in the larger
community. Do you have any ideas?*

*Some of our ranch boys are pretty
husky. Think you can handle them?*

*Most of our kids will finish their
education with the twelfth grade, or
at best spend a year in our junior
college. What kind of a program will
you offer them within the larger
curriculum?*

He knew what his teachers' strengths and weaknesses were:

*We've never had a good debate
squad. Yet the board has the money*

41

*to send them on trips. How'd you like
to spend some?*

*Several years ago the sophomores put
on a play and took it around to the
elementary schools. Are you
interested?*

*The school paper almost won an
award a few years ago. Since then,
well . . .*

The relationship between our CT and the superintendent, begun in this interview, remained a creative one. At closer hand, his relationship with the principal, who had taken over the present superintendent's former position, was another matter. But the superintendent kept a sharp surveillance over the high school's instructional program and personnel matters in general, and the creativeness continued for about one year.

However, even this alliance did not allow him to release his inventive powers entirely. Again, he returned to the wellspring of out-of-the-school pursuits which had provided the acceptance, sharing, and stimulation which the school environment and its administrators did not.

One activity was his association through his students with two very prominent, open-minded old families who understood what a boon his lively program was for their children. They sensed his sincere enthusiasm in two of the lasting interests in the community: ranching and gold mining. He was invited out to "ride the range" and also to investigate the cavernous depths dug into the side of a hill labeled "Esperanza."

Reflections.......................................

The masochist in him wondered whether he really deserved the rich feelings, the satisfaction he got from his close associations with students. Perhaps he was—as he imagined the principal's perception of his successes to be—immature, nonprofessional, too familiar, and not able to play the authority role from behind (not in front of) the teacher's desk.

.... End Reflections

Although some administrative resentment of his popularity with a small group of students developed, he was for the most part allowed some freedom to create with and for his students. Trips to nearby Hollywood were sanctioned. Two of his students had auditions with major film studios. A budding author had his play produced. Another, an almost illiterate student, won a statewide Lion's Club speech contest, a major achievement and a testimony to his conviction that there was a creative spark in each of his students waiting to be stimulated and released.

V was a ranch boy in the valley, but his roots had been nurtured on a farm in a state far away. His folks were happier but tenant farmers still, raising chickens for a large combine of poultrymen. V worked faithfully doing the myriad chores in the not-yet-light-of-day so that he might catch the school bus at 5:00 A.M. School was a haven, a resting place for his body and, unfortunately, his mind as well. Not that V didn't try. But there wasn't much in either hereditary or environmental background to help.

They met—our hero and the desert rat from Desert-O—and began a sequence of events which called on the creativity of each, marred not at all by the distance between their origins—the sophisticated East and the deprived hills of a downtrodden state.

Scene 1

V Can I try out for the speech contest?

CT (surprised, hesitatingly) Why not? Do you have a speech ready?

V No.

CT Well. (pause—long) Have you tried the library for ideas?

V No, but I will.

Scene 2

CT (catches sight of V in the library, *Liberty, Reader's Digest, The Farm Journal* in front of him) All contestants will submit their speeches by next Monday, please.

Scene 3

CT (reading the entries, comes upon V's) WOW! It doesn't make sense. Sentences here and there but disconnected, each with its own thought. Doesn't care what comes before or after. Is there even the finest of spiderlike threads of ideas here? Yes, but not much to build on. How did he do it? Sat down with one idea—freedom in our country—and wrote sentences almost at random. But something else is operating—his feelings about being free and about his country. That's the glue that holds this together. Not on the paper but in his mind. Can I help him see the pattern in the isolated sentences? Now *I* would put this sentence here, that phrase there. Cut it out, you yakkety-yak teller! Get *him*

43

to do it. It's not *your* thing. What do you want to do? Take the heart out of it? Resist! Desist! You jerk! Stimulate! Facilitate! Let V create!

Scene 4

CT   There is a beat in each of these sentences. Can you put the beats together into a symphony?

V   I don't understand. What do you mean—symphony?

CT   (to himself) He really *is* naive. Not even *symphony* does he understand. What *does* he know that I can compare it to? (to V) Like a flock of geese, flying in formation. Each one helps to make the wedge.

V   Oh, like in the autumn, flying south? I git cha!

CT   You WHAT?

V   Huh?

Scene 5

CT   (to himself) He's got a good ear. If I repeat each line, he'll get the rhythm and the intonation. Once he hears it he can repeat it. (to V) Wipe that *git, jist, gonna,* and *kin* out of your speech— NOW!

V   You becha, sir!

CT   Eh, eh, eh. Not ih, ih, ih, you hillbilly!

V   Oh, sir! Ah loved those hills back there.

CT   You WHAT?

V   Sorry, sir. Ah mean, I, I, I, I.

Scene 6

CT   Repeat, repeat, repeat!

V   Hoh K, hoh K, hoh K.

CT   Oh, my God!

Scene 7

Same

Scene 8

More of same

Scene 9

CT   (to himself) Will it ever be right? Hey! Hold it! Whose right— mine or his? Maybe, just maybe. Those "hill" roots. The country syntax. That twang!

44

Scene 10

CT   Well, V, let's get down to that auditorium and hear what it sounds like.

V   In that barn of a place? You're kidding!

CT   It's now or never. Go, baby, go!

Scene 11

CT   There! By George, you've got it! (to himself) Thank God! He hasn't lost the heart.

Scene 12

The local contest—won!

Scene 13

The regional contest—won!

Scene 14

The state contest—second place!

Scene 15

Photos in the local and big-city press. Plaques. Awards. Money.

No, he didn't go on to the national contest, but almost. And that *almost* was enough to remember the rest of V's life.

When V said it, he felt it. So did the audience—and more importantly, the judges. And after all the times our CT heard that speech, the tears insisted on welling up.

Reflections ....

The creative moment! A fairly creative atmosphere, our CT and his faith in a country boy, neither of whom forgot their sharing, that creative time together. Wild! Were there more such moments! And with more students!

.... End Reflections

Meanwhile, back in the classroom, our CT remembered all he had learned about establishing a positive personal relationship with some member of the administrative staff—superintendent or principal or secretary, in order to build a creative classroom atmosphere. Further, when he passed from his classroom into the hall, the school cafeteria, or teachers' lounge (often a dinky space in the boiler room), he knew, regretfully, that he had best leave any mention of creative activity or excitement involving students locked behind him.

Reflections...

Not only are unimaginative administrators the enemy of creative teachers. Colleagues devoid of innovative ideas or those whose creativity has been cramped may be hostile out of their own frustration. Talk of the excitement within a classroom arouses the envy and guilt of teachers who either have abandoned the creative muse because of constant or interminable frustration or who come to look upon their daily assignments as chores or work only.

.... **End Reflections**

Although no major battles for creativity occurred, there were skirmishes. For instance, the principal had shown little interest in the senior class play although rehearsals had been going on for weeks, every evening from seven to eleven in the school auditorium. It was understandable, however, since many principals come to their posts from the physical education department and are not overly concerned with the drama program. Thus, the request from the front office to submit a copy of the script came as a surprise.

During a conference the next day the principal suggested that the line, "She looks—pregnant" be cut from the production of *Junior Miss* by Field and Chodorov. Our CT might have made an issue and taken a stand against indiscriminate censorship. The students in his cast alleviated his ire somewhat by pronouncing, as they complied, that the principal was a square.

Reflections.......................................

The cutting of a line from a play is not the big issue but rather the relationship of administrator to teacher. The principal is responsible for the total instructional program. Therefore, this charge certainly must include encouraging the creative efforts of teachers, not merely criticizing, especially when initiated by outside forces. The principal should be so concerned and informed that any comment from the community could be countered immediately:

*I am aware of what CT is attempting
in his program. We have discussed it*

46

thoroughly. If you wish further
information, I will be happy to discuss
it with you at your convenience.

Too often he says:

> *Oh, I didn't realize what CT was*
> *doing. I assure you I'll check up on*
> *him at once. Thank you for bringing*
> *it to my attention.*

The tragedy of many creative situations is that the line of communication is so tenuous between teacher and administrator that the teacher alone is cognizant of the purposes and processes. His superiors and the community see only the product. That the first concern of the administrator seems to be the myriad of business details—budgets, buildings, and ballyhoo (Kiwanis luncheons, football booster clubs, etc.) and not the instructional program—the welfare of the students—compounds the tragedy.

This principal was simply not conversant with the long-range goals his creative teachers had for their groups—in this instance, drama: four major productions a year and the establishment of a community theater ready to serve students when they left school to continue (so all educators hope) to express their particular talents, repaying the community which has nurtured them for twelve years.

.... **End Reflections**

Not conversant, not concerned, and all mixed up about certain other relationships with and among his faculty, the principal's perception of the personal dynamics of the situation may have been somewhat biased by his feelings about that particular post as an interim one. His commitment to the staff and the desert community was not permanent. He was gazing at greener communities across the mountains and miles away from Desert-O.

Shortly after the *pregnant* episode, his interest in what was going on in that 7 to 11 sojourn in the auditorium was heightened by the fact that a custodian brought him word about discarded cigarette butts found there. He may have reflected:

> *Should I ignore the fact that CT is*
> *smoking in the auditorium during*
> *rehearsals?*

47

*What about the coaches and their
booster club pals? Are they smoking
during practice?*

*Can I insist that both CT and his
students not smoke during the long
rehearsal periods? Many ranch kids
have been smoking behind the
haystack since before puberty.*

*Can I bring the state law and
education code into the picture? What
exactly does it say, anyhow?*

Whatever he mused, our hero was hauled in for another session:

NO SMOKING IN THE
AUDITORIUM DURING
REHEARSALS!

CT's turn to reflect:

*Should I shorten rehearsals and come
up with a less-than-satisfactory
performance?*

*How can I leave 30 excited youths by
themselves for a ten-minute break
without destroying the continuity?*

*Come to think of it, no other faculty
member has volunteered to sit in on
rehearsals. Wonder why?*

*He'll never appear here in the
evening, that P. Just have to be more
careful about those butts.*

*Does he hand out the same dictum to
the coaches? They're constantly
snuffing out smokes when kids come
into the office.*

Our CT made only an unquiet peace with his administrator. The
conflicts of interests continued and convinced him that while some
creative forces were at work within the system, he had never totally
realized his own ingenuity. Sniping at his actions and programs
increased. Funds either were not available or magically disappeared
from the books. Also, he was criticized for associating with some of the
more progressive groups in the community such as the Mental Hygiene
Association.

48

And there were deeper turn-offs. When the position of curriculum director was created, he applied, feeling confident about his qualifications. Although he pushed the speech and drama program at that school, he had been a history and biology major. He had taught math and general science. His English major he had picked up in graduate school. He could feel the entire pulse of any school and could rap with colleagues from all departments—always a generalist, never *just* a specialist at the secondary level. But he had forgotten one thing: no administrative or supervisory credential on his record. On other occasions, on other campuses, he knew that administrators often encouraged teachers to get that credential. Sometimes they put them on the job without it but with commitments to finish it later. But not in Desert O. Therefore, no consideration.

Even inventing opportunities for advancement bore no fruit:

How about letting me help to orient
the new teachers, meet with them in a
few seminar sessions?

> *Surely. Sounds like a good idea. I'll*
> *let you know when we can set it up.*

It *was* a good idea, so worthwhile that they paid a consultant from a nearby teachers college a goodly sum, $300, to come and rap with the first-year teachers.

And they could have had me for
nothing!

And so he moved along, sometimes speedily, sometimes buffeted by hot-air blasts from administrative channels, sometimes becalmed by morasses of red tape. Had his relationship with the hiring superintendent continued, his chances at the department chairmanship would have been good. But as the district grew and the superintendent's duties increased, their association weakened. At the same time the young principal was beginning to feel his oats and exert more authority. Not in his plans was the promotion of our CT to any administrative, more equal position.

Reflections.......................................

Out of luck, baby—again. And again and again? Forever, maybe?

He paused. He reflected. Previously, he wasn't much given to pausing, just pushing on and doing—for kids. They turned him on. He turned them on—and on and on. But he had made new commitments in his personal life—a wife and child. They gave him pause, and pause he did.

49

What was his scurrying about all about? Maybe he could not find what he had so long been seeking. Maybe he had found only that plateau he was now resting on. Maybe he should plan to stay.

And yet . . .

It had been there from the beginning. Even that first-grade teacher had come under his scrutiny, and all the others who followed had been dissected by his evaluative eyes. This one was a "good" teacher; not so that one. And more and more he had come to reason why. The process had never stopped. It was his breath of life, the constant examination of the teacher role. This one communicated; that one did not. The other teacher shared, accepted, and stimulated. Over and over in his brain the same pattern was repeated.

Somehow, imperceptibly, this plateau seemed to shape itself into a pinnacle. Slowly he perceived himself as poised for flight. And the answer came. It moved him at once into that space which would become his new life style:

Teach teachers to teach!

Thus the goal, and the pathway to it: release as well as fulfillment. "Release? From what?"

Much of his near-past experience had been successful and stimulating. There wasn't an empty room, a blank wall that he couldn't transform into a learning experience. Not a chance remark from a student in his class, from a colleague across the lunch table, from the latest issue of an educational journal that couldn't blossom into an imaginative approach to some problem within the learning situation or the school system. And deep inside he realized that what had made it more successful and satisfying was his own inner happiness within his newly formed family circle.

The activities he generated may have created new scenes and inspired hitherto turned-off kids. But it was his thing, on his own time and only for him and his students. Those others downstairs and in the outlying buildings couldn't have cared less. But he wanted them, teachers and students, to care too—broadly and deeply. He spent hours advising one of his colleagues as to how he could develop communication with his students:

Don't take those derogatory remarks
personally. You are only a symbol, the
authority figure against which they
must rebel if they are to grow.

He consoled a student with literary aspirations in the young man's struggle to maintain an identity foreign to the ranch kids. Our CT

50

read his poetry and encouraged him to continue writing.

Somehow the system had to be changed. But where? By what means? In the above two cases, concern for colleagues should have been automatic with the principal involved. And individual interests, no matter how far removed from the desert scene, should have been recognized by counselors who were directly responsible to the administration. His own approach, deeply felt and honestly surveyed, was of longer range:

Teach teachers, or those who would
be teachers. Maybe I can show them
how to keep their faith in kids, and
practice it too, even when they move
up the ladder from back-office
classroom to front-office
administration.

It seemed to be the place to start, and any start after his experiences in upstate, on the boards, or across desert flats would be a step forward.

They still stood there, those stultified and stultifying administrators, after the many confrontations—resolute, immutable, unimaginative.

Am I getting paranoid?

After listening to the tales of woe from his colleagues, from students who tried to buck the system and failed, from deep within himself, he decided he wasn't. He heard the clarion voice:

They have declared themselves your
enemy. Face them, and they are yours.
Run away, and they will go on
forever.

He was running, not away from but to—to a possible solution to the problem by helping those neophyte teachers develop defense mechanisms that would bypass, defeat, and destroy, if necessary, those disbelievers in creativity—the administrators and especially that one called principal.

Damn them!

If he needed more ammunition to bring them to their sensibilities, he'd go out and find it—in research, discussion, and carefully planned strategies.

After being rejected or ignored, he looked no longer down those blind alleys. To be sure, he had been happy with his students of the desert valley and gave them as much of his creative self as conditions permitted. He had found both personal happiness and professional despair and so was not completely embittered. Among the past associations were

51

those individual students—the Ninas, the Bills, the Jiggs, the Donnas—who had become not merely roll sheets and report cards but rather huge concentric circles of acceptance, sharing, and stimulation.

.... **End Reflections**

Chapter 6

A Wonderful Thing Happened on the way to Elysium...

Reflections..

No CT can ever walk away from the haunting memories, the excitement of discoveries shared. No matter that principals and superintendents do not see or hear or feel the pulsations of lives that for a few moments of intellectual and emotional encounter meet and meld and grow. Because both students' and teachers' lives are enriched, no permanent bitterness ever overcomes him.

.... **End Reflections**

Our CT walked away, but not far away, from memories sweet and bitter to an involvement that he hoped would initiate and demand all of his creative energies. From experience he knew how to arouse in himself that inner curiosity which, in the process of satisfying it, would result in learning and personal growth. All he needed for the moment was that new situation where he might find those stimuli that would sustain his new resolve until he could function on his own.

He traveled over hot desert roads and icy mountain curves and smoggy, crowded freeways, miles and miles, to accumulate the necessary units which might fully liberate his creative spirit. But in the process he did not find the creativeness he sought. Oh, there was relief in new faces and associations but not complete fulfillment. He found instead that the same administrator, who arbitrarily managed public school systems, rose à la the Peter Principle to administer the university and became even more arbitrary and powerful and less creative in his entrenchment. He might have retired from a school district with enough of a fund to be able to afford the luxury of participating at the university level:

Superintendent's salary prior to retirement—$20,000+ per year.
Superintendent's retirement salary—$3,600 per year
Beginning Assistant Professor's salary—$7,000 per year
Professor's retirement salary—$0.00 in most private colleges without retirement benefits

Or perhaps he had walked away from those battles with the voting constituency to become a commander in collegiate seminars, urging neophytes to do battle with the threatening enemy he had retreated from:

> *Now when I was superintendent, this is the way I handled those rightist groups. Of course, we lost the election, but . . .*
>
> *I always backed up my principals. Whatever they said was it. This long-hair business and dress codes. I told them how to handle it.*

The professors were not much better than they had to be. They often expounded in class about this or that school district's problems:

> *When I surveyed the science program at ____ High School, I told them their entire department needed reorganization.*
>
> *That valley is really booming. Real estate values have tripled, so if any of you want to invest . . . I always like to pass this kind of information on to my graduate students.*

Reflections..

Professors' rewards for knuckling under to their fascist leaders are often in the form of such administrative plums as consultant fees. University administrators often have incestuous connections with school districts. Deans sometimes cajole former associates or friends to make consultant fees available to professors.

> *I've heard that Superintendent ____ is having difficulty with his school board. What that district needs is a team of experts to recommend a complete reorganization of their administrative staff.*

But the teachers in the district are insisting on pay increases. Where will they find funds for consultants at this time?

> *Don't worry. They've earmarked funds for them.*

Students learn of these nefarious practices as classes are canceled because professors are traveling on official business, which is never the students' business. Students may drive seventy miles one way to attend a seminar, only to find a note on the classroom door:

> *Dr. ____ will be in Hawaii this week to accredit ____ High School. Class will meet next week at the same time.*

Again, the shafted student is denied contact with the primary information source which is siphoned off for noninstructional purposes. The professor may be an expert teacher who is forced by economic circumstances—the low pay offered by most collegiate institutions, but particularly the private ones—to take on consultancies in order to make a living commensurate with his experience and status. This may be forgiven. But the incompetent one, the goldbricker who joins the university staff as a pedagogic means to the consultancy end, cannot so easily be forgiven as he stands or sits before his students in lecture hall or seminar room, stultifying further the creativity of those doctoral candidates who had so hopefully expected to garner creative wisdom at its pinnacle.

.... **End Reflections**

Delays set in as our CT's professors traveled to conferences at home and abroad, as they took unannounced sabbaticals. He shuddered to hear his colleague tell about his former try at completing a dissertation

55

when all the members of his committee died within the five years it took him to complete his writing.

He sat, listened, writhed impatiently in the uncomfortable chair and muttered under his breath:

More bullshit and more. Will it never
stop piling up?

What does he know about what really
goes on in today's public schools? He
probably spent all his predoctorate
years as a professional student or
taught only three years in WASP's
nests.

When was he last in a classroom,
anyway?

He had learned the system well. He programmed his thinking units into the noncreative but productive patterns necessary to persevere in and outwit the system. He sat, took notes, read extensively in the literature, and wrote papers with ideas that he knew the professors would agree with. Occasionally, he was excited by ideas from his fellow sufferers, especially their opinions and scuttlebutt about school districts:

Our district is going to try the
nongraded elementary school next
year.

We're building a computer center at
our junior college.

I hear that State College is expanding
its education department and adding
staff like crazy.

He also learned of the institutions of higher learning to be avoided, which of them was the lesser of the uncreative evils:

Did you guys know that at ____
University each professor has to
bargain with the dean for his salary?

Talk fast, and you'll make it.
Stammer, and you stay at the same
salary level for another year. And
that ain't much.

And he was able to generalize about private versus public colleges. Although some salaries at the former were considerably higher, they were usually assigned to "chairs" or were subject to the whims of the deans. At least the latter's salary scales were set by law and, although usually lower, were consistent.

Much, much later, he had some painful lessons concerning the personal differences of professors on dissertation advisement committees. Their opinions reflected against him when he unwittingly showed a preference for one or the other:

> *He needs more statistical data.*
>   —Educational Psychology advisor,
>   the statistician
>
> *I recommend another course in
> counseling.*
>   —Counseling advisor
>
> *The curriculum aspect needs
> expanding.*
>   —Curriculum advisor
>
> *But he's only measuring training
> background.*
>   —Teacher Education advisor, his
>   only ally

After the many miles, the many words and the countless hours spent in conferences, the battle finally over, he figuratively put out his shingle:

HAVE Ed.D.: WILL TRAVEL

But having a degree to travel did not automatically mean that there was a professional road to go down. And the application forms he filled out and the interviews he completed did not open doors at once. In fact, he was beginning to compute the cost and question the gain. And after several discouraging experiences he again paused and reflected:

*Mostly it has been this way in my
teaching career. It always seems more
difficult for creative teachers to pass
the interview test—that all-important,
initial impression.*

*Something about the enthusiastic
approach of a divergent personality
frightens a convergent personality,
whether principal or personnel
director. Each or both of them must
have swallowed system pills.*

*Even at that first moment, inquiring
minds are a threat. Administrators'
eyes, their tight-muscled faces, their*

57

*rigid bodies speak what's on their
minds.*

> *You fool! Why can't you recognize
> that you have reached the level of
> your incompetence? Relax and revel in
> it! I have. Why can't you?*
>
> *Why do you make me feel guilty? I
> won't hire you. I'm afraid to have you
> near me, reminding me all the time.*

But this time, for the first time in twenty years, it was slightly
different. He didn't have to call and call them. They called him. That
first recognition of his potential was to sustain him for a long while
and to continue to spark the above-and-beyond efforts that both helped
him internally yet worked against him externally.

It came—the historical moment: the dean of one of the institutions
he had applied to called him.

*Our computer goofed and double
enrolled a class. Could you come
quickly and help us out?*

It meant leaving the degree factory, the university, and really selling
what he had known he had to sell since graduating from elementary
school. And instantly all the creative surging welled up inside him to
produce the ultimate challenge: as a teacher of teachers, he had to
inspire them to the excitement he himself felt every day upon entering
the classroom. Each teacher candidate he even touched with his enthusiasm had to, in turn, stimulate hundreds of other students. How many
youngsters would he affect?

During the first months of our CTP's (creative teacher-professor) new
assignment there was an acceptance, a sharing, and stimulation which
spelled creativity for him. An associate professor was delighted to have
him, once she approved his credentials, to take over one section of her
favorite course:

*This is the way I have organized my
semester. Here are the assignment
and instruction sheets. I know you
have ideas of your own, but these will
give you a springboard.*

*Oh, by the way, if you want to hear
the best man in the business elaborate
on developmental tasks in education,
our audiovisual department has some*

excellent tapes. And the unit on
secondary schools is well served by
this movie we own.

The notes and materials she handed him would hardly fit in the drawer of his one filing cabinet, and he was grateful.

Materials and *freedom! WOW!*

Another professor informed him of the most stimulating conferences and dragged him along, introducing him to everyone all the way to the hospitality room and back:

Say, CTP, I'm going to a conference
on ____ next week in ____, up north. I
think there are enough funds in the
travel budget. How about it?

A home away from home with stimuli from every corner of the state. It was the largest world he had imagined. And his colleague made certain that when he was introduced, something besides the names and handshakes were exchanged:

Haven't you heard of CTP? We were
lucky to get him on our staff before
you guys grabbed him. Come on. Let's
drink to that.
I nominate . . .

And before he knew it, our hero's colleague had got him on a state committee.

Meanwhile, back on the campus, he couldn't help but become involved in those telephone conversations at the same desk they shared:

If you'd asked me to report about the
characteristics of elementary teachers,
I'd be happy to accept that panel
assignment. But since the emphasis
will be on secondary teachers, let me
recommend my colleague, who just
happens to have written his
dissertation on that very topic. Would
you like to talk to him? He's right
here.

Materials, books, and notes in colleagues' offices were always available to him. The cramped quarters and small campus gave an antiproliferation atmosphere to the total school. It made no difference whether the

59

persons sharing an office were in the same department or not. Advice came from all to each. Elementary, secondary, and counseling and guidance personnel sat in the same four-by-four office spaces to exchange ideas, visit each other's classes, or invite each other to lunch:

It's just great the way you're providing such broad experiences for your students. They're already all tooled up to relate better to academic and nonacademic students, as well as those advantaged or disadvantaged—black, brown, or white—when they become counselors.

No secondary teacher can function completely without understanding the complicated games played by the principal. I do appreciate your asking me to bring in a panel of administrators to discuss this interrelatedness with your preservice students.

And can you get some of your recently credentialed students to come and rap with mine? You know, these 15- or 20-year men may have forgotten what it's like in the beginning, especially how much it has changed.

I'm having a speaker from the State Department of Education today. Wouldn't you like to bring your class in to hear him?

Let's go to lunch: I'll introduce you to that tricky little blonde waitress.

The luncheons and occasional dinners effected an interchange that was self-perpetuating. Only one small, inadequate cafeteria served two faculties on one campus. So they banded together and became the favorite patrons of the nearby spaghetti bar, where our CTP was able to really rap with both veterans and other neophytes:

Having principals use assignments to teacher-training status as political plums is disastrous to our student teaching program. If we could only select our own training teachers, our

60

*student teachers would really come
out ready to handle classroom
problems.*

*At our graduate school we had a
great thing going in our laboratory
school. Do you suppose we could
persuade our dean to petition for one
in the new building program?*

Suggestions by one colleague were elaborated on by another.

*These are the personal data forms I
have my students fill out the first
class meeting. It helps me become
acquainted with them faster. Wanna
use some for your class?*

> *Hey! That sounds great! And then
> follow them up with individual
> conferences that really stamp their
> unique personalities.*

*Why not do that at the end to see if
they change—attitudes, interests,
involvement—over the semester. I'll try
it that way and let you know.*

If interesting experiments were going on in one classroom, they were
shared by other classes:

*All my students like to give
presentations in their various subject
areas. For instance, my biology
students took blood samples of every
class member and had them look at
them under the microscope.*

*And then there was one time my
home ec students gave us the
ingredients and said, 'Here's the stuff.
There's the stove. Now cook!'*

*Why don't we try letting your history
majors teach my science class?*

*Boy! These exchanges sure give
students chances to see the functions
of other academic and nonacademic
areas which they'll never see after
they're employed. The only teachers*

they'll associate with will be in their
own subject areas.

Reflections...

A creative spirit is a moving, magnetic, spark-striking spirit. The light-ning bolt of creativity strikes without warning, so long as the environ-ment is prepared to receive it. A CT's inner conditioning says: "Stay awake! Watch for the spark!"

When two sparks meet, the flame is kindled. It burns on and on. Each idea enflames another and another until a chain reaction forms that can set the world on fire.

.... **End Reflections**

Our CT responded to the stimulating atmosphere by positive action. Before him sat those to-be-teachers of all the students he would no longer reach. He was determined that they would come to know the ingredients of creativity and would utilize them in their future classrooms insofar as the limits of stifled veteran teachers, advance-ment-bent administrators, and the bricks and mortar of their individual classrooms would allow them. He could hardly believe that he would be able to accomplish this extension at the college level, but he threw his energies into the program as if it were really going to happen.

Because the temporary campus was limited in area, it was possible for him to become acquainted with the various academic departments—industrial arts, music, physical education, history. But his involvement with them alone was not sufficient. In order to encourage creativity among his students, he had to pass on the responsibility of making such contacts to them.

He insisted that the students form committees in each of their sub-ject-matter disciplines and give demonstrations either in the classroom or at a location on the campus where their individual departments operated. For example, in the classroom the social studies committee simulated a Spanish mission with costumes and props and brought the unit to a culmination by piling all the students into a bus and trans-porting them to an honest-to-gosh mission, approximately three miles away, where they were taken on tour by one of the padres. The industrial arts students taught their unit on metal shop *in* the shop. Surrounded by the buzz of machines all the students made nameplates. Physical education majors had their fellow students line up around the swimming pool to demonstrate lifesaving techniques. Meanwhile, the instructor stood on the edge of the pool, evaluating the teaching techniques employed and shivering all the while in the chill December air. This was a climax to a series of demonstrations in the various subject areas. In this way all the students became acquainted with the other worlds of the secondary school.

Then the shock of reinforcement! Our CTP, a teacher still even though operating at the college level, was stopped by the dean of the school:

I've heard good things about your
teaching.

This small admission did more to encourage him than anything that had happened to him in the previous ten years. It convinced him that he had made the right choice of locale and scheme of operation. It inspired him to move into unexplored areas of activity which extended him beyond the classroom.

To begin with, he took on one of his favorite avocations, faculty clubs, even though his days were jammed with getting to know the new academic scene. "Social committees" they called them, and he arranged dinners for retirements and holidays, encouraging further the camaraderie which the smallness of the institution fostered.

Soon, one of his colleagues sensed that he had other creativity—awaiting stimulation. This senior realized our CTP's sincere interest in students by virtue of his classroom activities.

You're a pretty good initiator and
facilitator. Why don't you see whether
we can get a local chapter of the
student-teachers' association started
here?

Our hero grabbed the idea and ran. He started with only a few students, those of the busy commuter college who showed real commitment and willingness to put in the extra hours beyond classes, student teaching, family, and part-time jobs. He dragged them to conference after conference. They repaid him and the college by getting themselves appointed to state offices and by going to Washington, D.C., as representatives to the national convention. They brought glory to themselves and their alma mater although the rest of the student body was unaware that anything beyond the next quiz, class, or lecture note was going on.

The outcome of these two acts stimulated his own extension of creativity even further. One of the criteria for promotion, besides instructional competence and professional activities, was clearly stated: "Contribution to the local community." His new locale boasted a unique theater group whose history began during the Thirties. It produced only original, unpublished, or unproduced scripts. Those playwrights

63

who couldn't make the Broadway scene—and who could besides Miller and Williams?—were offered, through competition, the opportunity for production. He wanted a part of that creative action. Starting as an actor, he went through the apprenticeship of director and producer and wound up president.

This time the bit was creativity generating creativity rather than escape from an uncreative atmosphere of the educational scene to a survival environment of community theater.

In addition, a small organization stressing rehabilitation of released mental patients utilized his speech training by asking him to address their groups. His audiences began with five or six members, and they rapped warmly and easily from the first. But they increased to one hundred or more, necessitating a style change to informal lecture. Finally, a reporter from a big-city daily who covered a meeting rewarded him with a lead article and photo, tangible evidence of his creative efforts.

And so it went, creativity pouring over and through all his activities—professional, social, personal. Preparation and luck coincided to provide an academic haven on earth where his restless, challenging, creative spirit found its home again.

Reflections..

This particular moment in our hero's career can be clearly delineated. The elements are integrated and dynamic. And since progress in creativity within the present educational system needs analysis of the positive as well as the negative forces, let us generalize the individual components that contributed to cohesiveness and communality, both of which gave rise to innovation.

The physical plant was small, the buildings few and close together so that intercommunication among faculties and facilities and administrations was easily maintained by a walk across the way. A face-to-face, first-name-calling kind of inter-relatedness was possible. In fact, there was no place to go but close.

Then too, the numbers of people and ratios of organizational components—students, professors, administrators—were small, making close interpersonal relationships possible. The fewer students congregated but did not swarm. It was easy for a professor or a student to walk through or into a group and call at least a few of them by name. Students and professors were so well known to and remembered by each other from one subject field to another, one semester to another that conversations could be picked up where they had left off weeks or months before. New raps could be initiated without time-consuming and polite but meaningless opening chitchat. Also, some of the faculty and many of the students lived near the campus, and it was not uncommon for an instructor or student to offer his home for a semester-long or one-shot meeting.

Another factor was the slow, careful orientation and assimilation of new members to the components. Administrators and faculty members in various disciplines who had worked together in close quarters for some time constituted a core that reflected the morale as well as the rationales and operation of the college itself and expressed its goals in fairly similar terms. All newcomers soon learned that most professors were educating students for the teaching profession. They saw their superiors and colleagues giving students the most relevant tools to work with regardless of the subject-matter area in which they were involved. The nucleus provided a backboard against which newly hired faculty and staff might evaluate themselves, a standard to react with or against.

The curriculum was another facet. Basically traditional, it was also extended, experimented with, moving out of a well-established and highly respected center. The essential stability gave professors the opportunity to work at once individually and collectively within and without the program of studies without upsetting the total program. There were room and opportunity for conservative and radical procedures under the same academic roof, as well as respect for and interest in followers of any learning paths, well worn or unknown.

Perhaps an even more important aspect, at least for our purposes here, was the administrators' awareness of all activities. Their offices lay cheek-by-jowl with classrooms. People and conversations of all kinds drifted in and sifted out along with the papers and more public concerns. Everyone ate in the same cafeteria at the same time; and chairmen, deans, and the like heard and saw what was happening at the more social noninstructional level too. They were able not only to listen to and talk over problems but act quickly, sometimes on the spot, on suggestions and complaints.

Lastly, there was that esprit de corps, an interwoven communication/action syndrome among the individuals and organizational components which said it all:

*We're young, maybe awkward, but
healthy and husky.*

We're together, attacking problems.

We create for common goals.

And of this all, our hero was a part.

65

Chapter 7

... But a Terrible Thing Happened on the Way Back

Our CTP never saw him, the principal, and P never saw our CTP. But he had an almost catastrophic influence on our hero, now a lowly assistant professor of education, trying to compensate financially for the salary loss he had suffered in moving from a high rank on the public school pay scale to the lowest rank at the teacher's college. He was teaching an extension course in the desert community where he had had his last job.

Reflections.......................................

Extension courses at most colleges and universities are a service to isolated communities, bringing the latest findings in educational research to those teachers seeking the most recent information in learning theory and techniques to utilize in their classrooms. Such benefits to teachers impose additional burdens on the professor. First, there is the added teaching load. Second, he must travel a considerable distance from the mother-campus. Finally, he is required to do the bookkeeping, making accurate records of attendance and fees.

In a sense, a professor, especially one on probationary status with the college, struggling financially, aspiring to work with graduate students who teach high school youngsters, must also *be* the college or university on the public school campus, where classes are usually held. On the other hand, the administrator, elementary or secondary, plays a background role only, rarely visiting classes or involving himself in the total process.

Our hero had some trepidations about how he would be received, since his students were former colleagues of Desert-O. He was delighted to see familiar faces and catch up on the gossip; they were equally delighted to see him even though they associated with him this time on a not-quite-equal basis.

The course was titled, "Problems of High School Students," and he certainly was familiar with the problems—and with the students. He also knew what his chores were: to give his teacher-students something to help them in their day-to-day activities with *their* students. Having lived through it himself, he knew their teaching problems as well as their sacrifices in adding more hours and effort to their already burdensome schedules in order to complete their credentials. As he had had to do, many of them, already certified to teach in other states, had to take additional courses to meet this state's credential requirements.

He had taken the lead in accepting them; they had responded. He shared his information; again they reciprocated. His next job was to stimulate them to contribute. And they did, the most obvious contribution—their students:

.... End **Reflections**

*Do we really know what their
problems are? From their point of
view?*

> *Well, they talk to us, rap about lots of
> things.*

*What things? Their cars? Their
friends? Their girls?*

> *What have those things got to do with
> school?*

*Do they have any influence? How can
we find out?*

> *Maybe we can ask them? Maybe
> they'd come and talk to us, talk with
> us.*

67

*Would they come? I mean, they might
think it's some kind of trick.*

*Let's find out. Will you ask some of
them to come?*

Sure. What can we lose?

Into his framework of lectures on research, distribution of dittoed bibliographies, and film showings our CTP injected the heart of the course—three panels composed of different kinds of students. The first group was college-bound, motivated, and secure:

*What do you consider the hardest job
for you in school?*

*Finding out what teachers want and
then giving it to them.*

*Have you read any of the Great
Books?*

Maybe. Which ones are great?

The second group included not-quite-committed students, wavering between ·the goals of college and work:

*What will you do if you don't have a
high enough GPA?*

High enough what?

*Grade point average. To get into the
university.*

*I dunno. Go to work for my old man,
I guess.*

Have you thought about JC?

*Junior College? I don't know much
about it except they have a good
basketball coach.*

The panels were enlightening and enjoyable for both teachers and students. And the professor and his class looked forward eagerly to the third group—the tuned-out, turned-off, rebellious near-dropouts. For the session our CTP brought along a film about dropouts, focusing especially on an adolescent's struggle with his feelings of sexuality.

During the first half of the three-hour class the students talked openly and easily with the group:

*What bothers you most about
teachers?*

*They're always yakking at us, telling
us what to do. Why don't you just act
like people?*

What *should* we *be doing?*

*Listening—at least once in a while.
You don't even* want *to know about
us.*

*How can we listen to your troubles
and still get through the courses of
study?*

*They're a big nothing, a waste of
time. Why don't you mix them up,
make 'em history and English, science
and math, so we can have afternoons
for work.*

*Like wow, man! Let's mix it up. Make
'em. Let's have intercourses! That's
my kinda work.*

Cool it, fellas.

*Well, you asked us to tell you what
we think, didn't you? We are, dad, we
are!*

It's about break time. How about
some coffee?

Sure, dad. Excuse me. Sir.

After the break everyone settled back as comfortably as possible in
the miserable classroom seats, designed for no human's anatomy, for
the viewing of the film. Two or three teachers lighted cigarettes, and
the projector rolled. One of the students waved the instructor to
his seat:

*Can we smoke, too? Just cigarettes, I
mean. OK?*

Reflections.......................................

At this moment a creative teacher might be distinguished from a noncreative one by his words and actions. The NCT (noncreative teacher)
remembers *first* the official rule constantly broken by adults in the
same setting—no smoking allowed. He probably would answer briefly,
and with little compunction:

Sorry, no!

69

Our CTP's thinking, always divergent and geared to weighing alternative risks, was different:

*We invited them. They have shown us
that they are sensitive and
responsive—and crude—but real.*

They have endured and contributed.

*They are rebels. They smoke at home
and in the school's restrooms. And
more than cigarettes.*

*They have learned that one set of
rules applies for adults, another for
kids. They see the teachers smoking.*

*They are not far away from
adulthood: jobs tomorrow, the draft,
perhaps death.*

*Smoking might fit into this behavior
puzzle somewhere.*

*How can we reward them? What's a
reward anyway? Something you want,
right? What do they want? Can we
give them what they ask for?*

.... **End Reflections**

He approached some of the teachers:

Whadaya think?

> *Gee, I don't know. Why ask me?*

Why not?

> *Well, I'm not sure.*

His decision was not an instantaneous, capricious one. But he made it, as always, in favor of the young blood with whom he empathized. No hassle. No big deal. No one really made anything of it.

The course ended successfully as far as our hero, his students, and *their* students were concerned:

> *Hey, it was a blast! Us telling
> them—and them on the hot seat.*

I only thought *I knew my kids.*

70

*How can we possibly teach subject
matter when they're so wrapped up in
themselves?*

LATER

Across the desk of a not-too-highly-placed, not-too-friendly-appearing extension official came a letter—to be forwarded to the president of the college. It was signed by the principal, not the on-site one where our CTP had given the course but the principal of an adjacent high school from whence had come some of his teacher-students. One sentence stood out like an italicized, capitalized phrase of pornography:

*HE FORCED THE STUDENTS TO
SMOKE!*

Our hero was further accused of inciting high school students to immorality. On the surface it appeared to him an insult to his sensitivity. But it was even more viciously a condemnation of the entire adolescent culture:

*Goddam son-of-a-bitch! He's so
ossified, stupid-blind drunk with his
own importance he probably doesn't
even know where kids come from.*

*He wouldn't know the teen scene from
a gang rape—and he lives in it all
day long!*

*Doesn't he see? Doesn't he hear?
Doesn't he care? Socio-pathic m-f!*

He was so incensed that he was ready to storm the president's office immediately, breathing fury and invective, to denounce the secretive back-biting action, to demand a full-scale hearing. And maybe to lose his job, too. His quest: to do something about the insidious, unrealistic, dehumanizing system.

He lucked out, perhaps for the third or fourth time in thirty years and out of hundreds of confrontations with front offices. The kinder heart and cooler head of the administrator prevailed, this time extending sympathy first and caution later, until our hero wound down and finished his litany of tongue lashings. Only then did he advise him:

*I know it's slanderous,
unsubstantiated. You've every right to
be p-o'ed about it.*

71

*I'll be damned if I'll let that stupid
bastard get away with smearing
professional careers by spreading
malicious lies!*

> *Easy does it, CTP. You can be sure
> that the letter will never reach
> President ____. I won't bother him
> with it.*

*But once that bullshit is in print,
baby, it's hard to silence.*

Because his boss had accepted his vituperative outburst, as well as
shared his outrage, our hero felt that he had established some confidence
about his abilities and competence with the higher-ups. He believed
the man. The acceptance and sharing by administration, by that time
never to be expected of supervisors, stimulated him into action, to
initiate his own protective device.

*If I can't clear myself in the open,
maybe I can be just as sneaky as that
pompous ass flexing his power-hungry
prerogative.*

*I'll clear the kids, my students and
myself, in case it ever comes up.*

*I can throw my weight around too,
you piddling pipsqueak. And I think I
have enough weight to do it.*

Back to Desert-O he traveled, not once but several times, to solicit
his teacher-students' alliances in a mutual defense pact:

*. . . and that's the whole bit. Would
you believe?*

> *I'm trying. God knows, I'm trying.
> What are you going to do?*

*I need notarized letters from those
who were present, stating that at no
time, by no pressure, were students
forced to smoke.*

> *Where do I sign? And have you
> talked to ____ yet? He'd back you up
> all the way. What about the kids?*

*I've wondered about them. But I don't
think so.*

Yeah. I feel that way, too.

The matter was never exhumed.

Reflections..

Although the protagonist and antagonist of this slight but significant drama never saw each other, the villain of the piece, the principal, evidently heard some rumor (amazing that he even found time to listen to one of his teachers) about the incident. Without requesting an interview with the professor or writing for an explanation, he penned his vicious, untrue accusation. He forgot the common decencies of direct discussion, the innocent-before-proven-guilty concept, and the professional ethics that his own personal or professional training should have taught him.

The idea of developing communication between teachers and students by the use of student panels was a creative activity. Any principal, aware of this problem so prevalent in secondary schools—students' and teachers' inability to reach across age and experience gaps—should have been grateful for any assistance providing some solution. Instead, he proceeded to direct action without considering the effects that his letter would have on either the professor or his teachers.

The problem is one of allegiance. When the question of morals of teachers and students arises, who shall be served first in order that the educative process, not to mention the creative one, be fully operative: teacher to student or principal, principal to teacher or supervisor?

A conflict exists in the initial organization of all educative institutions. In a hierarchical instrument that retains the authority figure at the top, educational institutions attempt at the same time to instill a democratic, self-reliant ideal in those who attend. Each process apparently nullifies the other. Not only students but teachers, laymen, everyone is beginning to question this paradox.

.... **End Reflections**

Chapter 8

Creativity Concreted

For five years the unique features of that particular institution where our CTP functioned as an assistant professor served as stimulators. He came to know many of the staff personally, contributing to many cooperative, creative projects. For instance, the faculty of the School of Education re-evaluated the entire program of teacher training, attempting to answer the two most important questions:

1. What is a good teacher?
2. How can we help to create him?

Also, they initiated a Participation-Observation program to bring teacher candidates closer to the students earlier in their schedules, placing them in schools as teacher aides.

Then too, reinforced interpersonal contacts were planned by faculty committees. The Christmas open house sent some on their way to vacations abroad or close by. Book-warmings announced a professor's newest publication.

The inconveniences of the physical plant were shared, overcome, or ignored. During the hot, hot afternoons in nonairconditioned buildings the long break over coffee or coke eased the strain and made each one feel better because the others endured it. And the repartee in winter-cold buildings or on mud-washed paths was warm and easy:

Hey, man! Don't you remember?
"Make the students do as much of the
work as possible," you said at the last

74

*meeting. So how come you're lugging
that projector?*

*You treating the world all right?
Incidentally, my wife is concerned
about how your boy made out after
his operation. Everything OK?*

*Yeah, it's a tough life, but it's moving
and so are we—to a bigger house in a
better neighborhood.*

As expected, the first concrete structure raised on the new campus
comfortably housed the mechanical, a heating plant for the boilers and
electrical equipment, while the human element suffered in temporary
buildings, freezing and sweltering by seasons.

Some professors complained about the cramped quarters, awaiting
impatiently those cold concrete cells which would divide them from
their fellowmen forever. But others recognized that creativeness was
possible despite or perhaps because of the confines of a space that forced
human beings to relate with other human beings in a communal-type
structure.

Our hero, like all of the other soul brothers before him and now,
made the best of the worst of things. He hobnobbed with the elite,
those academics—professors of science, English, and mathematics—who
ordinarily avoided those lowest on the totem pole—educationists, or
professional educators. He forced them to listen and forced himself to
listen to them. His remarks were deliberately naive in order to elicit
a torrent of words. He cornered them; he challenged them; he parried
and thrust with them. And in the close quarters of the dining room
there was no escape for them—or him:

*Why should our students majoring in
physics have to take education
courses? They know their subject
matter.*

*But they have to learn, along with the
physics content, the insides of kids
and how they learn.*

*Can you cut down the number of
education units required for high
school teachers? We'd like to boost
our majors from 30 to 60 units.*

*We have only 20% of their time now.
Whaddya want—blood?*

75

*Anyone who can read well and pass
our comprehensive exam can teach
English.*

Can pass your *exams maybe. But will
they pass the exams of their teaching
ability, especially when their kids test
them?*

Then occurred the onslaught. The portent of the end of the creative spirit was in the air. Various publics demanded more and more educational opportunities. Throngs of GI's, who had spent one weekend in San Diego, Hollywood, or San Francisco, wanted to extend it into a lifetime of relaxed affluence. The way led through the many educational institutions available. Blacks from Mississippi and Alabama who saw the dismal road ahead educationally in their states, as well as braceros up from Mexico, were quick to grasp at the almost-free education offered by community and state colleges.

Legislators responded by providing resources in terms of bond issues and direct allocation of funds to state colleges and universities. Industry was booming. Educated personnel in both technical and business fields were desperately needed and might be best trained in the community, by state colleges particularly.

At his own home base our CTP witnessed a tripling of buildings, staff, and clientele in the ensuing five years. Concrete structures on a site across town, briefly assigned the romantic name of Paloma, began to rise. Where once small bungalows had stood loomed five-story monolithic giants:

Where can we meet?

Where can we eat?

Someone finally remembered that perhaps a cafeteria would help in a building housing 5,000 students and staff. So they superimposed a penthouse-type eatery without the accoutrements: for example, no kitchens. Catered food had to be hoisted in the one elevator that served both staff and salads. It wasn't very conducive to chatting with colleagues—no soft lighting, checkered tablecloths, or familiar waitress. It was strictly serve yourself, plastic utensils, tissue-paper napkins. Grab the food. Eat it. Beat it. There was no lounge either, no gathering place for gossiping or rapping or crying. No reserved john or even a selective pot to pee in. The physical factors worked against camaraderie. And he writhed. Undefeated, however, he stuck his head into a hundred offices: "I'm CTP. Who the hell are you?"

76

At least it eased the pain.

Reflections.....................................

Can concrete cremate creativity? How is it possible that in the move from temporary to permanent structures a faculty's creativity can be stultified, buried under tons of crumpled rock which man has used to cover the earth? CT's dare not look over their shoulders lest even fond memories disappear.

Somehow concrete monstrosities cannot foster that creative climate forcibly induced by proximity of body and breath and being. Newly erected, freshly painted exteriors bespeak at first glance sterility and uncreativity. Unfeeling, irresponsible architects should be chained to their works, to be fed nothing but old nails, blueprints, and bowls of concrete mash.

> *It's only a school.*
>
> *It'll be better than any school I attended.*
>
> *I'll get that contract even if I have to cut out every unique feature.*
>
> *It was good enough for me. It's good enough for them.*
>
> *I'll build that dream school next time.*

And so the struggle goes: to maintain the creative spirit engendered in a small nucleus of claptrap buildings with communicative, enthusiastic experimentalist like-minds. Perhaps this is the secret that nature saves for those who would destroy her:

Verywell.
    Buryme.
        Layerupon
            Layerme.
                Change my features from green to gray.
                    Smother me.
                        Defile me.
                            Enshroud me.
                                Try to destroy me, the
                                  fount of creativity.
                          But I shall deceive you,
                      Corrupt you,
                And in the end destroy you,

You uncreative spirit.
For what you have come from
Cannot be denied
Nor prostituted.

.... End Reflections

And as the physical plant took on institutional proportions, professors and administrators moved to more comfortable but also more distant quarters, isolated by steel and space from their former conversants. That president who had reigned over the temporary campus moved with great pride to the new concretized setting. But he had great difficulty keeping in touch with his rapidly multiplying family. From one office from which he could shout into the next and get an immediate response, he moved to a complex of offices where it might take hours to reach that secretary whose boss was responsible for the building phase of the program or the personnel operations or the instructional area.

When requesting advice from various administrative arms such as counseling or registration or placement, and after three telephone calls instead of the previous one, our CTP might locate and talk to a human being:

This is CTP. Is Miss B there? Oh?
When did she get transferred?
American Studies to Associated
Clinics to the Dean's Office—in two
months?

Well, is Mr. C in? He's gone, too? Oh,
the whole office was moved? And no
telephones installed yet, huh?

Yes, I'll talk to Dr. D. Maybe he can
come up with some special procedures
for this student who's in my office
now and really needs help.

WHAT? The _____ Committee has to
determine procedure now? And they
don't meet till next month?

How about Dean E. You mean to say
he's . . . When was the funeral?

But inanimate buildings and administrative build-up and shake-up alone did not silence our hero's creative spirit. The academic organization factor also played a large part. Devisive departmentalization shut off

78

the interdisciplinary exchange, that basic force that educates the whole person.

It began fairly slowly, the disintegration, as one by one the departments were transported across town to that former peak being whittled down to a noncreative plateau. Departments within divisions grew until the latter became schools within the largest framework, the college. And each of these grew by additional faculty, at least one hundred per year, so that schools took over entire buildings instead of merely a few more rooms.

Ironically, it was decided early in the plan that although the book building was to be called LIBRARY and the chemical building was labeled SCIENCE, no building was to be designated EDUCATION. A school it was—School of Education. But it could not aspire to have that name carved or brass plated into the cornerstone of any towering think-tank.

So science moved away from education, and our CTP heard no more about the great nature-study trips planned for zoology students. In fact, as a member of the secondary school department he was no longer certain that anything happened to kids before the seventh grade. Elementary education had dropped to a lower floor. And that was that.

The departments within the School of Education itself began to exert their various pressures—elementary versus secondary, administration versus counseling, etc. When he consulted professors in other departments within the school, our hero began to feel guilty, bound as he was by allegiance to his own department. If colleagues in other sections solicited support for policies that might be deleterious to his own department, he felt compelled to vote the party line.

He eventually found himself on a curriculum committee whose responsibility it was to concern itself with the college as a whole rather than departmental aggrandizement. It was the only place on the ten-acre site where the friendly faces, which had begun to recede for lack of encounter—out of site, out of mind—came back into focus. But those formerly open faces he used to meet around the luncheon table began to take on a more reserved, set look around the conference table, then a hostile look as the battles for space, students, and status heated up. He often felt himself knuckling under but more out of long-range gains for the students and the total college than the immediate growth of his department:

This curriculum change will clobber
my students, won't get them where
they're headed for still another
semester.

79

But it will be great for those starting
next fall. And it sure will jazz up the
_____ courses, make them much more
valuable and meaningful for the
students.

I vote aye.

The added burden put on him, the trust of colleagues who elected him to preserve their sovereignty, pushed him painfully into the reality of the moment. In dedicating himself to maintaining a climate wherein students might develop their own creative dynamos, his own machinery, so enthusiastically received by colleagues in the old setting, was in danger of sabotage.

As he marshaled his thinking and finally his decision and raised his hand for aye or nay, more often than not supporting his department, his reflections stuttered, faltered on the word *student:*

Why can't I make my decisions and
cast my vote for what I perceive to be
in the best interests of the students?
Who in the hell ever thinks about
them?

But his words were loud, and often angry:

All I hear is courses, credits, and
curriculum. What about the students,
for Christ's sake?

Have you buried the students in the
concrete, too, or will they just
disappear in the verbiage of the
catalog?

The compromises reached—an increase in the number of units for various majors, the determination not to offer science laboratory courses in the evening, did not add up to that really creative dynamic he had hoped might be retained from the earlier structure. He remembered most vividly the name change—from _____ College of Applied Arts and Sciences to _____ State College. To our hero, part of the creative spurt that had come with the acceptance by the newly hired professors of the former name, that of serving a segment of the socioeconomic student population newly enfranchised educationally, was being abandoned, at least in spirit:

After all, nurses, teachers, librarians,
policemen, and electrical engineers

*are as valuable as Ph.D.'ers in history
and English, doctors, and lawyers.*

*Why do so many of us aspire to turn
out so many eggheads when the world
needs so many knowledgeable and
human technicians?*

*And where are they now—in the
70's—those Ph.D.'s? Adding prestige to
bread lines?*

It was almost inevitable, considering the delicate threads of interlocking obligations and interests that any organization is tied together by: jiggle one strand and the whole web trembles. Thus even individual professors became obsessed with the possibility of private empire-building within the total and departmental structures. As middle management became more concerned and preoccupied with administration rather than with instruction, professors became pivots in the power-play game, spending hours formerly dedicated to cooperative, progressive efforts in jockeying for positions which involved them deeply in political shenanigans.

> *Let's vote Dr. E into the curriculum
> committee. He'll battle down those
> empire builders of the _____
> Department.*
>
> *I've got to propose that course for our
> department and get it through the
> three committees or we'll never have
> an _____ Department. Can I count on
> your vote: and in exchange for what?*
>
> *If Dr. F gets on that promotions
> committee, I may as well start looking
> for another job.*
>
> *Those two committee members have
> doctorates from the same university.
> Watch out for their thrusts, and don't
> forget to parry.*

Some of the more enterprising professors saw the burgeoning institution as a threat and fled to smaller ones. Little did they know that the disease of size and inhumanity would follow them. And the brain drain saddened our CTP because he knew that some of them were irreplaceable. For a time he maintained a communication with them, but even that was severed eventually.

81

Reflections..

In large, self-aggrandizing institutions each professor's department becomes the most important ingredient in the college functioning. By gaining advantages and success for it, he accrues peripheral glory for himself. And so he fights desperately to gain every advantage he can for his small empire, at times at the expense of the rest of the college operation. He cares nothing about his colleague's contributions to creativity or the ultimate benefits for all students in the total program. If his department gets its share, he also gets his. And eventually he comes face to face with the true hierarchy:

Me

The Department

The School

The Administrators

The College

.

.

.

The Students

.... **End Reflections**

Another delicately balanced facet suffered irremedial damage. The unique and productive program inaugurated by some of the staff at the former campus diminished as administrators and less responsible professors strove to compete with universities, which followed a more traditional curriculum. The arguments began:

Of course an experimental approach
such as no grades, pass or fail
courses, would be terrific.

> *But graduate schools won't accept our*
> *students unless they have A, B, C,*
> *grades.*

Gee! That new on-site program is
really great—where the action is!

> *Without statistics we'll never attract*
> *funds from foundations for research.*
> *And you can hardly quantify interests*
> *and attitudes. At this rate we won't*

82

> *even be in the running against*
> *universities, state or private.*

Why do we need a doctoral program
that copies ____ University when what
public schools clamor for are
innovative Masters' programs?

> *We've got to begin on the doctoral*
> *program now, even if it takes ten*
> *years to develop, or we won't even be*
> *a dot on the collegiate map.*

Why build an annex as big as the
original library if the shelves in the
old one are only half filled? And what
junk! Nothing new for the past ten
years in the ____ section.

> *The difference between a college and*
> *a university is the number of volumes*
> *in the library.*

The more realistic difference in programs and procedures between universities and state colleges had a tap root in professors' perceptions of state colleges as primarily teacher-education institutions. The educationists, those concerned with teacher education, were very aware of what was happening in public schools. They had taught in them, had kept up professional and social contacts with former colleagues, and listened eagerly to and questioned their students about activities, feelings, and personnel in surrounding school districts. On the other hand, the academics, especially professors of history and English, had come directly out of graduate school into collegiate teaching.

Reflections.......................................

Face it: academicians come to the end at the end of the graduate road.

> *Now what do I do? I thought I was*
> *going to write that Great American*
> *Novel.*
>
> *I was sure that ____ Publishing*
> *Company couldn't wait to grab me as*
> *an editor.*
>
> *Here I stand with it in my hand. Who*
> *wants historians? How many directors*
> *of historical societies are there?*

83

What these desperate ones need is jobs, and the only positions available are in state colleges. They grab them.

It's a start.

They still aspire, however, to university jobs—the salaries, the students, the status. But they're really trapped. They can't stand the demeaning sound of "state college"

"Could even be ___ Normal School."

and the nonreading, unsophisticated students at that level. And at the same time they don't want to face the competition that comes with university life: papers read at conferences; publishing; literate, demanding students.

.... **End Reflections**

Frustrated and in need of a target to vent it at, acade-maniacs took on the nearest available rival in the pecking order—the educationists:

> *Why don't you do a good job of training your teachers? These high school graduates are so dumb they don't know their elbow from their asshole.*

Can you help us develop better methods classes?

> *I've got my own responsibilities. You rework the program. It's your job.*

How about supervising your majors in their student teaching?

> *Public schools are the last place I want to be.*

Junior college maybe?

> *They're just as stupid. If we got our students as freshmen instead of juniors, we'd shape them up.*

How would you teach those beginning courses?

> *Jesus Christ! Me? Teach lower division? No way! Let my grad students handle them.*

Reflections.......................................

There is an added dimension that influences this dichotomy. From time to time state legislators alter requirements for credentialing. They feel compelled to reflect the "public's" interest—as though they cared. At such times schools of education must retool to meet the mandates. Educationists are always active in fighting for or against various bills in assemblies and senates and cases in courts. Academicians are rarely affected by legislation or legal decisions and precedence. Nor would they sully themselves to enter such ungenteel frays, even if their interests were threatened.

In reality, they are so seldom cognizant of the world outside the concrete cloister that only on-campus or community riots blast open their eyes. Then they quickly superimpose a catch-all course which looks and sounds all right in the catalog but has no content that evolves from the core of the subject nor meets the needs of students who might enroll.

Nor do subject-matter–oriented professors hear the direct early warnings from students in their classes:

> *The most worthwhile values in a society have been learned by reading the classics.*

> *The kids in my area are pretty straight, and all they read is the* Free Press *and* La Raza.

> *Never mind what's going on in your neighborhood. Let's get back to Chaucer.*

Students who are headed for teaching in public secondary schools are aware, all the while the professor is rambling on, that what he is giving them will never turn on high school students:

> *What a bunch of crap! Who needs to know minor Elizabethan poets when the kids are mostly interested in grass and wheels.*

> *I'd like to see him operate with those thirty pairs of I-dare-you-to-'larn'-me eyes looking up at him.*

Not many college students are willing to jeopardize their grades or degrees by challenging professors about the relevance of the course content.

I'd better just keep my ideas to myself.
I wanna get out of here some day.

Further, teacher education is constantly revamping, combining, or experimenting with courses and programs even though the changes may not be imposed by law. Usually springing from action research, the shifts reflect, sometimes spearhead changes going on in public education. But subject-matter professors more often pervert student teachers' energies from the goal of becoming good classroom instructors. For instance, a philosophy department with no graduate degree program may seduce teacher trainees into a single course, promising to offer the full program in succeeding semesters if they will enroll in the beginning course. Or anthropology may dangle the golden carrot of overseas jobs, opportunities in the diplomatic corps, as rewards for helping the department grow.

In the end, too many knowledgeable teachers-to-be become involved in the acade-maniac drive toward departmental isolation and imperialism. And these are the very people who are destined to teach in establishments where accurate understanding of and equitable cooperation with others—administrators, colleagues, and pupils—are prerequisite to creativity.

.... End Reflections

Meanwhile, back in the lecture halls, the labs, and the seminars, a sadder but wiser Paloma watched as the combined impact of these three largest aspects—place, people, and program—left the product, the student, the greatest loser. Those 3,000 learners, soon to increase to 10,000 and then quickly to 20,000, longed for more permanent, more comfortable structures. What they did not realize was that they were really begging to be buried in the concrete along with Mother Nature.

Luckily, there was a nucleus of hold-out-and-hang-on professors left on the freeway campus who were determined that at least the human element would be retained as long as possible. The School of Education set up advisement hours and insisted that they be strictly adhered to. Students could always find a listening ear for those problems which increased geometrically as the concrete monstrosities rose high and higher. Because they were often the only cars around, education professors had to counsel in subject-matter areas, registration procedures, placement, even personal problems. They also encouraged students to decide for themselves how to balance and manage their employment and academic lives. And often their counsel was at odds with information the students received from their major advisors:

86

*If I take this ed course, will it count
toward my Masters in math? It might
help me in the classroom, but that
math course . . .*

*Any of the urban studies will help you
learn more about ghetto schools—and
their kids—before you even meet them.*

*Take the math course. You might
want to work for IBM some day, or
maybe teach in junior college.*

*I can't wait to finish this credential
work and get that job!*

*Great! Find out whether teaching is
what you want, what it's all about,
and which direction you want to go.*

*Do you wanna mess around with
students all your life? Get that
Masters so you can get out as soon as
possible.*

*What do I do now? They both sound
right.*

One thing at a time.

Go, go, go! Stay, stay, stay!

Thus, students resigned themselves to being urban college commuters with as little concern for the institution's social or moral status as it had for them. Their primary goal became getting into the track, persevering and emerging with the appropriate document—a union card which would admit them to practice whatever it was in secondary schools.

Behind and between these scenes our CTP moved and struggled all the while to forestall the inevitable demise of creativity. He met again and again with committees to battle against the overwhelming forces of geography and political maneuverings, all the stifling forces he recognized so well. But sheer numbers and power defeated him. A rigor-mortis-type divisiveness set in as more and more deans were added. Wedge-like, they widened the gap between the Big Dean and the professors.

Our hero, who had spent so much time and strength in the NOBLE CAUSE, slowly began to realize that he was standing all alone. He turned around and looked for them, his contemporaries in seniority, and finally found them several steps above him:

87

*For heaven's sake! How come they're
up there and I'm still here?*

*I've been standing here, fighting for
the students and didn't even notice.*

*I always thought that students were
the reason for our being here. But
they aren't.*

Neither the acclaim of students inspired in his classes sparked by meaningful activities nor publicity about other activities helped him advance. Others were promoted in rank, but not he.

Why not?

Why my colleagues and not I?

Where did I fail?

*Have I got to get on that bandwagon,
too?*

Though he sought the answer from his colleagues and his administrators, no one would divulge from that mystic cave, the promotions committee, the reason for his being left on the ground holding the ladder. All his former equals became his superiors, sitting stolidly and formidably on higher rungs. His efforts at self-analysis resulted in the sad, correct or no, conclusion that he had given too much of himself to students and not enough to his colleagues, now grown somewhat distant, status- and interest-wise, and their political machinations.

Unable to beat them, our CTP opted for subversion. He labored for three years with the curriculum committee, hopeful part of the time and also discouraged at having to compromise at others:

Seventy-five units for physics majors.

*But you'll never get enough teacher
candidates to take that many units.*

*But I thought you said you wanted
well-prepared physics teachers in the
schools?*

*Sure we do. But don't forget: this is
only the beginning teacher we're
talking about. He'll be back for his
Masters—if you guys treat him right.*

*Oh, a year in the classroom and he'll
change his mind, especially when ____
Oil will pay him three times his
salary.*

88

He finally won his promotion, which indicated that somebody somewhere cared. This rewarding response encouraged him to initiate and participate in an experiment, the first of its kind, in team teaching in teacher education.

Two colleagues, both as interested in action research *and* in promotion as our hero was, labored with him after-hours to set up a program that tried to measure the effectiveness of more than one instructor's viewpoints on one group of students. On the books were three sections of the same course taught at the same time by three different professors. The content included evaluation, curriculum, and principles of secondary education. Sometimes the sections met separately. At those times each professor did his thing: rap sessions, field trips, lectures, panels. Sometimes the ninety students joined to hear a speaker, watch a film, or listen to a lively debate among their three professors:

> *What is a "good" teacher?*

> *I say that teaching's an art. So does
> Highet.*

> > *But they're made, not born. Read
> > Skinner.*

> *It's the human personality you're
> talking about, and Sullivan says it's
> the other people around you.*

> > *We like to hear experts disagree
> > among themselves. It makes us feel
> > better and honors, indirectly, our own
> > points of view.*

> > *I never knew professors could lose
> > their cool in an argument and still
> > continue to work with each other.*

> > *They're like . . . like . . . human
> > beings.*

This activity was one of the greatest strengths of the three-year experiment, as the final evaluation revealed.

The students also expressed their enthusiasm about the effectiveness of an executive committee drawn from each class which helped to set up the program, reported to their classes, and generally provided a wide channel for communication among teachers and students. Another well-received innovation was the use of paperback books, about eight or ten, as texts.

> *Gee! What a relief from those tomes
> we usually have to lug around.*

*I don't know why, but I get more out
of these paperbacks, enjoy reading
them.*

The team itself was an agreeable synthesis of diverse talents. One provided involvement and insight, another more stability, and the third assorted practical talents in teaching as well as writing. The attempt, at first cautious, became bolder, more definite, and finally reality in operation. There were plans, there were students, and there was a successful feedback from all to all:

*Shall we present the Eight-Year Study
in detail, with lectures, slides, and
film?*

> *It's very important, but the newer
> research on the disadvantaged child
> takes precedent, it seems to me.*

> *Still, there's never been an experiment
> and follow-up like it. Shouldn't they
> develop an historical perspective?*

> *OK. Let's see if we can't make room
> for both by using closed circuit TV.*

The pleasant, productive feelings thus created stimulated each member of the team-taught classes to ask the question of each other almost simultaneously:

> *Why not write it up?*

> *For students everywhere who are
> worn out by the stentorian tones of
> one authority.*

*For others—teacher education
institutions—that might like to try it
out.*

> *For us. Remember our promotions.*

So write they did, asking during all the tortuous hours:

*Is it going to be possible to present
cogently our three viewpoints as one?*

Week after week—extra meetings not only for the continuous planning for the experiment still in progress but for the article that was to present their rationale and outcomes.

The end result was a worthwhile achievement: satisfied students, successful team teaching, and published documentation. The three rejoiced in each other's contributions, the good feelings they engendered. But as they walked toward the administrator's door with their purchased reprints in hand, each wondered:

Do they really give a damn?

Energy, imagination, plain hard work
we poured into it. No one shirked.
Everyone worked.

And the students cared. Wish they
were sitting on that G-D promotions
committee!

The creative experience, an exhilarating and exhausting learning task for them as well as the students, had raised not a ripple, scored not a scratch on the academic landscape.

A year later one of the team left to take an advanced position with another institution which agreed to immediate promotion as part of his contract. Another, also passed over for promotion, took a two-year leave to work with the federal government on a foreign project. The third, our hero, thinking he had moved away from the principal-teacher syndrome but finding it the same old chessboard maneuvering with new labels on the pieces—dean-professor—stayed to try the game one more time.

Reflections ....

Promotion in any racket—business, politics, the military—is a crazy four-step operation called Get It:

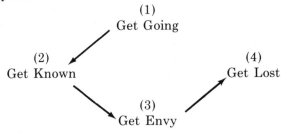

At all levels in all types of schools, advancement usually means more time—for refining skills, for reflecting. A department chairmanship means an extra conference period, presumably for department obligations. A move from the classroom to the counselor's or VP's office, for the full day or a period or two, means more time for helping young people with problems which keep them from doing their best as students. Coaching, leadership, library, or in-service teaching often frees a teacher

91

from a full class load and allows him to pursue his own development while providing needed paraprofessional services.

The coin received, however, requires reimbursement. At the college level, for instance, promotion may relieve a professor of continuing to teach extension or junior college courses. But more often his hopes for a slower pace dwindle before the upward rocketing of the cost-of-living index, a growing family, a more affluent life style. Advancement may also relieve anxiety, the battle for recognition, but only for a while. The next step soon brings on the up-me-ship urge again.

Ego-enchancement is a natural outcome, of course. But it, too, extracts its price. A devisiveness sets in, inexorably separating teachers and administrators. One class of personnel appears more successful than the other by virtue of status, income, and power. Self-satisfaction is often bought at the price of camaraderie, cooperation, and companionship despite each's protestations that things are the same as they always were. To himself the achiever says:

> *I have met the majority, and they are*
> *mine.*

Perhaps.

.... **End Reflections**

Well, action research in instruction
doesn't seem to ring bats out and
bells in administrators' belfries. What
can I try now?

The real thing, the doing—no!

Maybe they need the baffle between
them and reality. They can't stand the
classroom, especially if it swings:
students, teacher, curriculum,
methods—the whole bit really
grooving.

The baffle. Hm-m-m. Intermediary.
Language.

A book—Sí?

He and another colleague, who taught the same kinds of classes, were in the process of choosing a new text. After reviewing a hundred of them and finding omissions in all, they decided to write their own:

What could we say that would be
different?

92

*With so many books available, we
probably won't have much chance for
publication.*

*What about collecting all the
differences?*

        *It sure would be easier to collect than
to write.*

Selected readings seem to sell.

        It's fairly new.

*My students love controversy among
supposed experts.*

        Paperbacks are a big hit with mine.

Right on!   *Right on!*

They got it all together, sold it to a publisher and received good reviews. Success again—sort of. Their students used and liked the book. But even the authors-organized bookwarming hardly made a stir, despite free booze. The college's house organ gave it one line—no reprint of reviews, no congratulatory acknowledgement. Nobody home. It was more than a year before the promotions committee got around to granting it recognition and its authors additional stars in their promotional crowns.

Again, one left for other fields; our CTP remained.

*I've got to get away, too, before I go
out of my gourd. Even a short break.
Maybe a permanent one.*

Like an answer to a desperado's prayer, the opportunity dropped in his lap almost before he crossed himself: a six-month Fulbright fellowship abroad. Before his next breath he signed himself up and left for a greener-pastures vacation.

The change left him refreshed and revitalized. He always felt that way after new experiences. Most of them were successful because he willed it that way, perhaps because there is no other way for divergents—plain CT or gold-plated CTP.

He returned to the former frustrating scene renewed, excited—with photographs and write-ups of accomplishments, and mused again:

*A new president of the college might
be different. Maybe this one will
listen.*

*I do owe something to those people.
WOW! The promises I made!*

93

*He ought to be impressed—or
interested, at least.*

Portfolio in hand, he knocked on the president's door and entered,
rhapsodizing:

*Look at this. What a set up! Each
Spanish major at State could
translate one of these ed books from
English into Spanish—look at the
stacks of them—as a Master's project.*

> *Hm-m-m. I see.*

*An overseas campus. Our Chicano
students would love it!*

> *Ah-hm-hm.*

*Here are faculty publications. Great
stuff here, but it needs to be
translated into English before we can
use it.*

> *Well, the chancellor's office takes care
> of exchanges.*

Reflections.......................................

It figures. Standard Operating Procedure: college style. Cut off. Abort.
Creative teachers may be tolerated, accepted. But they are seldom
shared with. And they are never stimulated by:

> *It looks interesting. Let me see what I
> can do.*

or

> *I can't be of much help myself, but I
> can tell you who to see.*

or

> *Let me set up an appointment for you
> to see ____. He would be interested
> and much more helpful than I.*

Caretaking covers a multitude of administrative sins. It screens out
the fact that communication, acceptance, sharing, and stimulation in
the educational world is a one-way street. Changes, improvements, and
advances never seem to come. And the changes are almost always

94

convergent, rigidifying, establishment solidifying, thereby throttling grass-roots-born, imaginative practices.

Administrators may be glad creative work is going on and may even give it a modicum of tacit approval. But by and large little concrete evidence or acknowledgement of it in others ever flows from those in charge: no money, no rewards, no offers of assistance, even denial of association if the project is in danger of sinking.

No higher-ups ever visit to observe imaginative process. No one cares about results or even comments, congratulates, or castigates the developers. Nobody seems to know that things are going on, that experiments are successful, that innovative programs have value to the schools in terms of providing new insights into the students, not to mention turning a PR spotlight on how the taxpayers' dollars are being spent.

Administrators can capitalize on goings-on in many ways. Press releases describing and evaluating activities can be sent to news media. Schools can offer many services that utilize staff, facilities, and programs to surrounding communities. Educators can also verify experiments by expanding programs within their own schools or by testing them in others.

But if the administrator isn't aware of the specific activities his staff is engaged in, neither his superiors nor the community can know what's happening.

In reality, when students, teachers, and programs lose, even the house doesn't win.

.... **End Reflections**

95

Chapter 9

Of Course,
If You're A Risk Taker...

Our CTP's duties, besides classroom teaching, included what was formerly called teacher training—the supervision of student teachers (ST), sometimes referred to as cadet or practice teachers. In the field, a public secondary school, in a classroom filled to overflowing with thirty or forty students, he could observe and assist soon-to-be full-time teachers.

Reflections.......................................

Between his academic and professional education course work and probationary employment, the ST functions directly under the guidance of a classroom training teacher (TT), a permanently employed staff member selected by the principal, for at least one hour each day for four months. The ST appears to others, and to himself, at a creative peak after years of intensive, extensive exposure to the educational process. All his energies are focused on that class, that ONE class alone.

During this training period he is observed at least once a week by a college supervisor (CS), a former secondary-level classroom teacher who is also an expert in the particular subject-matter area. Besides these two supervisors, ST may be visited by a subject-matter specialist in the school district and very rarely, if at all, by the principal of the school. If he is judged competent by all of the above, the college placement bureau recommends him for certification by the state.

.... **End Reflections**

Our hero, now CTP-CS (creative teacher professor-college supervisor), was determined to facilitate the on-going development of CT's, to smash barriers so that his students could move freely to cultivate their creative powers:

No one, no way, is going to break this
chain I started in my campus
classes—not administrators, not
classroom supervisors. No body!

Reflections...

Oh, no? Easy, baby. Don't blow your cool.

.... **End Reflections**

After a year's experience supervising in one district's schools and noting the worth or worthlessness of TT's, our CTP-CS was assigned to another district. He had always asked and had been granted his request by the cooperating teachers: that his ST's get at it right away since they had spent many hours observing in classrooms just prior to their assignment as ST's. But he soon discovered that his charges had to observe their TT's in action for three weeks before they were allowed to appear "on stage." The announcement had been made at a tea reigned over by the constantly smiling supervisor of student teachers.

CTP-CS advised his charges:

Maybe a week of watching. Then try
easing yourself into the scene. Slowly
and carefully.

But it came out, as reported by TT's:

You'd better let ST teach or else . . .

Reflections...

Ready for this?

97

A supervisor, assigned from the school district, to place both elementary and secondary ST's, coming from elementary environs where tea and cookies were the only social lubricants, Smiley complained, objected to the intrusion of new ideas and procedures, to the college coordinator of ST's:

> *He can't tell our teachers how to do their job.*

The word filtered down to CTP-CS:

> *Back off. Do it their way.*

After all the past defeats incurred when he charged head on, this time our hero superficially bowed to higher whims, then tried outflanking maneuvers. Here and there he found cooperative conspirators who were willing to let ST's take it from the top. In time, more and more TT's came around to the same way of thinking.

Except one.

She was not only an authoritarian personality in her own classes but even more arbitrary with ST's. Our CTP-CS went through the bit of suggesting, cajoling, and catering to her in order to protect his student as subtly as he could:

Could you help him try a couple of days of the new grammar approach?

> *The department believes in three weeks of strict grammar drill. He's got to follow that form.*

OK. I see. Yes, you're right. Your experience could be most helpful to him.

He supported his ST as best he could:

So. She turned down your idea for socio-drama? Well, write it up, present it to her again and let her mull it over.

> *Why bother? She'll just red pencil it.*
>
> *And she's put the kibosh on my unit exam, too. Wants me to use her old tried and true one.*

Offer to run off enough copies of yours
for her third period class. And don't
forget to make her an answer key.

He tried not to sacrifice his own creativity entirely but finally gave up in disgust. Knowledgeable CTP-CS and innocent ST suffered together until the experience was finished.

He thought that the situation was closed at the end of the semester. But the administrative hand had struck again.

Reflections..

From *HANDbook for Administrators,* Chapter ____, "Communication":

No, No's	*Always's*
Confront underlings:	Go directly to their superiors.
Meet their superiors face to face:	Use the back door, especially by telephone.
Speak above or below AD-MINI-TALK:	
	Generalize: ". . . meaningful learning . . . individualized instruction . . ."
	Rationalize: "didn't make the list but ____ put in the good word for him."
	Disguise: "Area . . . ADA . . . target school . . . OEO . . . printout . . ."

.... **End Reflections**

This time Smiley went straight to the top—the college department chairman, and a new one:

Who does he think he is, pressuring
my teacher?

CTP-CS's department chairman passed on the bad word to him:

You'd better go make your peace with
her. You've got to live together.

99

Her smile couldn't mask her body language—taut, unmoving, up-tight in every nerve:

> *The problem is between the training teachers and the student teacher.*

Hell! TT knows the teaching racket. He's safe.

And ST will learn soon enough what it's really like in those foul frontline trenches, the stinking classrooms of some ghetto school.

God damn it! Our business is to help ST, and to protect him as best we can while he learns the ropes.

She'd never heard it so straight and must have thought:

> *How dare he use that tone, that language with me.*
>
> *Do you suppose he's going to attack me?*

Her thoughts generated her action. She wept:

> *In twenty years I've never had any problems.*

Our shocked, unbelieving CTP-CS tried to soothe her and then backed out as unobtrusively as he could.

Soon afterwards an outside administrative consultant team from a nearby university analyzed the total downtown office. They recommended that Smiley be kept in her position. She began taking short leaves of absence, then longer ones. He went on supervising, but it was five years before he was able to re-establish his former rapport with all his TT's.

Reflections.......................................

Perhaps this incident might be discounted as a confrontation affecting only an administrator and a CTP-CS. But another event occurred several years later which impinged more drastically on an ST and his TT. It is related here as a defense of and a warning to all the vulnerable ST's taking that first step into a classroom as a sort of junior partner.

.... **End Reflections**

Conditions hadn't changed even though our CTP-CS had become more experienced and highly respected by the administrators of several school districts. And the ST involved in this case was clearly a creative personality. He had been observed in college classroom situations. For a methods class he had shot footage of billboard advertising. He showed it to his classmates, indicating how they might use it in lessons on propaganda, art, and cultural history. He had also been an apprentice in a teacher-aide situation in a ghetto school, where he directed young blacks in a scene from *Midsummer Night's Dream* rewritten in ghetto language. The lines were very clear: he had proved himself to be an accepting, sharing, stimulating teacher candidate.

Our hero felt most confident that the student teaching experience for this young man, whom we shall call Innovator, would be a rich, rewarding one both for him and the students under his direction. And the TT, chosen by the principal in order to release her for administrative duties connected with her position as department chairman, seemed to be an accepting personality. We shall call her Veteran.

The weeks went by, and as predicted the entire experience was a satisfying one, especially for the students:

> *Man, I dig on this poetry bit.*
>
> > *Yeah. 'Richard Cory' goes down easy with ____'s rock music to go with it.*
>
> *Jeez! I can't write an essay about what I was really thinking during the quiz. I'd get suspended for life!*

Each time CTP-CS visited the classroom, Veteran assured him that the students accepted Innovator, that he shared his knowledge and experience with them, and that he stimulated them to valuable learning activities:

> *The students relate to him very well.*
>
> *His presentations are always well planned with considerable resource material.*
>
> *He uses a variety of audiovisual material to keep their interests alive.*

BUT: The Tragic Flaw:

> *He uses incorrect oral grammar when addressing his students:*
>
> *"There is two sets of books on the shelf."*

*"I want two sets of papers from both
of* youse.

"We'll read two chapter *for
tomorrow."*

"Many of you hasn't *turned in your
themes."*

Shocked, disbelieving, CTP-CS visited again and again, listening with
ears that could hear a pronoun drop. On no occasion did he hear what
Veteran claimed she heard. Further, he remembered the many other
occasions when he had heard Innovator speak: his methods class where
he gave teaching demonstrations, his apprenticeship in the ghetto school,
several individual conferences with him, informal conversations with
his peers that our hero chanced to overhear. Never could he recall any
misuse of the English language by Innovator. He investigated further:

*You've known him for several years.
What do you think of his speech?*

> *It's like any other English major's.*

*Have you ever heard him use bad
grammar?*

> *Golly, no! And we English professors
> are more picky about that than
> anybody.*

> *I surely would have noticed if he had.*

Nonplussed, he returned to Veteran with his findings. She remained
adamant:

> *Oh, he's a likeable enough fellow, gets
> along well with students. And he does
> have creative activities.*

> *BUT . . .*

The confrontation finally came on the day that written evaluations
of Innovator by Veteran were due. When she was handed the forms
to complete—those forms which would make or break Innovator's opportunities to get a job—she refused to write anything:

> *I will not approve an ST who cannot
> use the king's English.*

Our hero, foolish Don Quixote, arranged a conference with Veteran.
After an hour of analyzing the situation with her, he was defeated by
her adamancy:

102

You admit that he could be a very
effective operator with young people?

> *Yes, but not if he uses a singular verb*
> *with a plural subject.*

Wouldn't you write an evaluation
which would include both strengths
and weaknesses?

> *Well, perhaps . . . but . . . no, no.*

Do you realize that this may mean
the end of a career for him, one for
which he has prepared for five years?

> *But it's admitting young men such as*
> *he into the profession which weakens*
> *the entire fabric.*

His only other avenue was a direct appeal to the principal:

You must admit that Veteran has
passed her prime and that she may
have become too . . . ah, ah . . . rigid.

> *We need more people like her, those*
> *who can maintain our standards, are*
> *stable and reliable and reflect the*
> *expectations of the community.*

Couldn't you write something on the
evaluation to indicate the impasse
with her?

> *Me? Write an evaluation of an ST?*
> *That's not a principal's function.*
>
> *There's no reference to it in the*
> *administrator's policy booklet.*

Couldn't you try to persuade her to
change her mind?

> *What? And lose the only person who's*
> *willing to head the department next*
> *year?*

Oh, yes. P was sympathetic. He agreed to discontinue using Veteran as a TT in the future. But there was nothing he could do about the evaluation. Vested interests defeated them both.

The upshot was that Innovator was given another assignment in another school, where he did so well that his second TT personally

103

called principals all over the district to get him a job. He got one, and he proved himself a hundred times over during the years.

However, it was not the end of it for our CTP-CS.

Reflections..

One more time.

.... **End Reflections**

He discovered a variant. Some administrators, besides being uncreative, were also vindictive. When the next semester began and he was to return to the same school for supervision, he found that he had been transferred to another school district. Questioned, his department administrator finally broke down and admitted that he had received a telephone call from the principal involved in the Innovator-Veteran episode, merely the insidious message over the wires, the sum of the revelation:

> *We had some trouble over here last year.*

No letter. No details. No opportunity for defense:

What did he mean by trouble?

> *Well, you know . . . If he doesn't want you, he doesn't want you.*
>
> *He's done this before. Did you know that ____ can't supervise there anymore either?*

He's not going to add me to his list of "unwanted's"!

> *Don't worry. It won't be on your record. We're the only ones who'll ever know.*

But there are other phone lines to other offices, higher even than yours.

What guarantee do I have that it stops here?

> *Oh, now, see here!*
>
> *I'll give you an easy assignment at a beautiful WASP school—no problems.*

104

No sale. I want a letter of
explanation with specific
charges—and reinstatement!

By himself and without any support from the college administrator, he confronted P directly:

If one of your teachers had a
complaint about you, would you expect
him to call the superintendent of
schools?

> *No.*

In the several years I have been
working in your school, have you ever
had any complaints about me as a
CTP-CS?

> *No.*

Then why did you lose faith in me to
the extent that you had to call my
supervisor?

> *Well . . .*

Then you really have no legal or
ethical reasons for denying me access
to your school, do you?

> *I suppose not.*

Then of course you would be willing
to state this in writing to my
supervisor?

> *I'll have to give it some thought.*

And I shall receive a copy of the
letter?

> *Hm-m-m.*

He waited—and waited—and. He checked with his supervisor:

Had a letter from ____ yet?

> *Not yet. How many times have you*
> *asked me so far?*

Eventually, one term's worth later, he received the weasel-worded retraction:

There is no reason why CTP should
not be permitted to return to ———
High School at this time.

Reflections.......................................

In the beginning there is the CTP-CS's grapevine:

Not one dissenting word, CTP-CS.
Your students have to play her as she
lays. And not a thing you can do
about it.

The pairing of teachers, ST's and TT's, depends in part at least upon the political position of the classroom supervisor within the school's structure. In other words, the most creative TT's may be easily bypassed if they do not happen to belong to the school's in-group. This means that the classroom supervising teachers who work with CTP-CS's and their ST's may or may not be those kinds of personalities who respond to creative designs. Therefore, CTP-CS admonishes those neophytes, who sit around him awaiting instructions before beginning their assignments, always in the same manner:

Your training teacher is the boss. If
he allows you freedom to create, fine.
If not, you must go the route.

> *What happens if we don't see eye to*
> *eye, if I want to try new materials, a*
> *new technique and he won't buy it?*

If you lock horns with him, you lose.
He may know more; he may know
less than you. But he's your ticket to
ride. Keep him happy.

Of course, if you're a risk-taker . . .

The crime of crimes it is for him to have to say it to every group of ST's:

Create! Create! But don't be creative.
Wait. Postpone. Put those feelings in
hock until you have your own group of
young people sitting before you in your
own classroom.

You'll be clobbered if you try—if they
even allow you to get close enough to
that job to get clobbered.

106

Of course, if you're a risk-taker . . .

And yet he is torn all the while—the pitting of the reality of the classroom against the idealism of the teacher education program environment. It is always there:

*How far should I encourage them to
extend themselves into the realm of
creativity?*

*When should they draw back into
that protective shell of conformity to
the system?*

He shows them, of course, both sides of the picture:

*Clear with the supervising teacher.
Play it safe—cool.*

But he wonders:

*If I even mention the alternatives, am
I deterring them, even puncturing the
bubbles of creativity?*

Of course, if I'm a risk-taker . . .

His conscience does not allow him to let his charges venture forth into the educational pandemonium unarmed, innocent, unsophisticated. If the blow were to fell his students, he wants to be standing there to catch them. He foresees the years ahead, at least that first year, when they will be piled upon with paper details, with record keeping and concern about discipline and order in the classroom. His neophyte teachers have to meet the future shock unaccompanied by any sympathetic listener, concerned superior, or compassionate colleague.

He knows how NCT's feel:

Don't baby them.

Sink or swim is the motto.

I had to, too. And now I got it made.

His own memories crowd in to validate their viewpoints—the upstate thing, the ghosts on the boards, the cigar-smoke–filled room:

*Not that. At least, for them. Not these
bright and shining candidates brim
full of creativity.*

*Maybe the warning will insulate
them, make them more patient for
that day when some administrator*

*somewhere will have the guts to stand
with and by his teachers, not against
them—know their names, ranks, and
employee numbers even.*

So he suggests connivances:

*Close that door and don't let anyone
but your students in on the secrets of
creativeness.*

*Share it with them and them alone
and at the same time warn them: "If
we get turned on in this class, keep it
to yourselves."*

*Present it to the boss in writing with
a carbon copy so that after he agrees
and signs it, you'll have it for
evidence: "He said I might be
creative. Here's the word he gave me."*

*Be circuitous. Around and around
him circle until he's so dizzy he
doesn't know what he's agreed to
really.*

*Then rush to your classroom and get
with those kids so that if it is all
turned off by the systems experts, your
students will at least have had some
creative moments with you.*

On the rare occasions when creative TT's are chosen to supervise
ST's, the selection is basically by default but sometimes by design. For
example, all of the principal's disciples may turn down the prospect
of training an ST:

*I don't want any amateur messing
around with my gifted students.*

*Fifteen dollars a month to let some
squirt and his new-fangled ideas
disrupt my classroom with group
discussions, play acting, noise? No
thank you!*

*It's too much work. I'd probably have
to have conferences with him during
my free period.*

*And you know I always play handball
with ___ at that hour.*

The principal, unable to pressure his hangers-on, perhaps out of honor among blackmailing back-scratchers, turns the vacuum into a trap, suckering in the unsuspecting CTT (Creative Training Teacher):

Now I'm stuck.

*Do I have to hand this plum to that
nonconforming, question-asking,
teacher-organizing bastard of a CT?*

He's the only one left.

*But on the other hand, it's one way to
put him on the spot. I'm sure he'll get
himself or ST into trouble.*

*Then I can legitimately clobber him
on his yearly evaluation.*

Perhaps there are other attributes—ingenuousness, optimism, a lack of bedrock suspicion—that seem to come naturally to CTT's with their initial acceptance of their ST's. The sharing of expertise—about students, subject, and systems—follows:

*I don't know whether you ought to use
that excerpt from* Catcher in the Rye
*on that class ditto. But go ahead.
Just don't identify it.*

*I don't know of any better example of
the search for identity that young
people face and want to talk
about—with someone, somewhere—and
right now.*

The stimulation might be pressured, a challenge from the initiator of acceptance and sharing to the receptor of them. Or maybe there is acceptance and sharing on ST's part, at least as far as CTT perceives him. In either case, he asks:

*Say ST. You have access to the ___
film library. You know, we can't get
half the stuff we want because of the
tight scheduling in the city's AV.*

*Our materials are so old, too, or so
nonexistent. How about your bringing
some goodies for your class to see?*

109

*And maybe I can show them in my
classes, too?*

> *Ah, ha! I knew he'd fall into my trap.
> Now I've got 'im!*

P calls CTT into the office:

> *Why did you let ST drag in a film
> that wasn't approved by the
> downtown office?*
>
> *Now I'll have to call the college and
> complain to the director of student
> teaching.*
>
> *This is not going to get you points on
> your record, you know.*
>
> *I don't care if the council of all the
> English teachers in the world
> approved of that book. We're not
> going to use it in* this *school!*
>
> *I don't have time to defend it in front
> of other principals even if you
> prepared the brief.*
>
> *Keep that pornographic garbage out
> of the classroom!*

In all fairness some choices of TT's include very competent teachers
who function well in the role. They are easy to spot:

The class is yours from now on.

*I'll be right here if you need me for
anything—finding materials, tutoring,
whatever.*

Too often, however, the appointments are arbitrary and political,
spoils for the groupies:

> *In case you want me, I'll be in the
> teacher's lounge.*
>
> *If anything comes up, I'm in the
> principal's office, helping him on a
> survey.*

It would also be unfair to say that creativity in public schools is
stifled only by administrators. The very organism to whom this author
has attached the word *creative* has also proved to contribute to the

110

un. The veteran teacher who plays the role of TT is sometimes also guilty. In a kind of cannibalistic reaction, ST's are often in danger of having their creative efforts attacked by one of their own.

Envy sometimes causes the reaction. A more mature teacher realizes that the usually younger ST may be more attractive physically, mentally, or emotionally to his students than he. His feelings set up a barrier which is implemented by his insisting on strict adherence to text, curriculum, or personal format. Thus, ST has little opportunity to put into action his own creative impulses. He has to go the route, try to squeeze himself into TT's mold.

Possessiveness is another of the several deadening sins perpetrated upon ST's:

> *This is* my *class. No one is going to take it away from me.*
>
> *I'd really rather do it myself.*

Once TT's make such statements, either orally or by facial expression, creativity slithers away to hide in the shadows, awaiting a sunnier day.

Ambition and sloth are also deterrents. The drive to become an administrator leads to practicing the role through arbitrary decisions and direct commands:

> *I've used this approach for years. It never fails.*
>
> *No, don't do that. Go march the band around the building. Be sure they practice that new step.*
>
> *Correct and grade these three sets of papers by tomorrow morning.*

Sloth involves moving completely out of the classroom to assist the principal in his duties and to neglect ST, ignore him completely UNLESS he can contribute something visible to the school's image:

> *The coach needs that backfield tightened up before our big game with _____ High. Get out there and help.*

Such vices work against on-growing creativity in any relationship, and especially in student teaching wherein only close-at-hand, consistent helpfulness can steady the trembling knees, slake the dry mouth, and stanch the flooding armpits of the anxiety-ridden, about-to-be teacher.

Besides the choice of TT's and their matching with ST's, there are other pieces in the pairing puzzle. For instance, no one in the college—

administrator, CTP-CS, or ST—nor anyone in the public school district—supervisor, TT, or pupil—has any part in the three-way merger of college and class supervisors and ST's—SAVE ONE—P. The principal, or his favorite matchmaker—vice-principal, dean of curriculum, etc., arranges the amalgamation. And not only do CTP-CS's, devoted to the sponsorship of creativity in their students, have no choice or voice in allowing uncreative TT's to become involved in the practice teaching. They also have no recourse to appeal in the event of a mismating.

An important corollary to the P: CTP-CS relationship springs from each one's perception of his role vis-à-vis the other. Creative CTP-CS's consider themselves teachers first and administrators (because of their supervisory duties) second. They move to the college level to continue the teaching function rather than to the public school administration level. Because they are primarily teachers, they are addressed by P in the same manner as the regular staff is:

> *We expect you to sign in when you visit, just as the teachers do.*
>
> *Would you mind using the pay phone instead of tying up the office ones?*

The objection here is one of principle. The supposedly equal relationship between P and CTP-CS—two professionals most concerned about accurate personality matching as a component of effective teaching—deteriorates into an authoritarian relationship with CTP-CS being dictated to and serving, in P's mind, as another staff member.

Of course, there are rare exceptions to this practice. The college supervisor may have come from administrative ranks, having made only a brief pause in the teaching ranks on his ascent to the principalship. In that event he is treated more as an equal:

> *Say CTP-CS (former P). Stop in the office. I'd like to know more about that district you retired from.*
>
> *Take it easy. You don't have to visit that ST too often. I've got him placed with one of our soon-to-be-administrator boys.*

But mostly there is a complete lack of creative cooperation—sharing—at a crucial time when the disintegration of imaginative human interaction can destroy developing creative teachers.

The keystone is P, almost invisible most of the time. Nobody sees him, not CTP-CS's, their ST's, nor *their* students:

112

I never met the guy.

> *Which one's P?*

> > *I never got into trouble.*

Waving his plum-laden wand over his unmagical kingdom, P rewards Kiss-Asses with TT assignments and disappears behind his desk barricade, leaving the pairing to whatever underling is in his closest favor. He seldom reappears and only when beseeched by special favorites—coaches, department chairmen, cronies:

> *Don't bother me about replacements now. Nobody's leaving till the end of the year.*

> > *Thought you'd like to eyeball that super-stacked broad in ___ 's drama class.*

> *Yeah? Check her out today.*

> > *That blood assigned to auto shop used to play fullback for ___ High.*

> *Change him to first period student teaching and tell him to report to Coach ___ for the rest of the day.*

> *If he's hungry enough, he'll work his butt off to get a permanent position.*

> > *I gotta hard guy who'd be great assisting in the boys' VP office.*

> *Set it up. But you know our policy about hiring his kind. Careful what you promise.*

In truth, P is overburdened with paper work and understaffed with paper shufflers. He utilizes his favorites' free periods for his own benefit, repaying them with assignments which increase their salaries. Another in-group usually comprises his personal friends who may or may not donate time and effort to his pet projects. They all get theirs while others, perhaps equally or more capable, perhaps not, get none, not even a smile or a cheering word.

Among his UNfavorites may be one who in reality is his best teacher. But if this creator is a staunch union member, P fears he will seduce ST's politically. Some people on his staff remain faceless, unknown blobs. But he knows CT's by their ego-threatening reputations and their busy, noisy, activity-filled classrooms. He hears too many complaints from

113

their neighboring NCT's who pass by on the way to the teachers' lounge or cannot keep their own students' eyes, ears, and attention from wandering away from his dull readings and lifeless lectures and wondering about the blast next door:

> *One more riotous classroom in this plant and I'll go out of my gourd.*
>
> *One more CT infecting ST's with their divergent poison:*
> "Think for yourself!"
> "Prove it!"
> "Choose!"
> *Not while I'm here.*
>
> *If CTP-CS comes charging in here, thinking he can throw his Ph.D. around, he'll find out fast who's in charge.*

Again, in the beginning, college supervisors, who know their ST's best by virtue of classroom encounters and weekly seminars during their initial teaching experience, are not consulted. Their opinions as to which ST's to place with which TT's are never asked. In the end there is no evaluation of TT's by CTP-CS's, ST's, P's, or anybody else. There is no feedback about effectiveness, efficiency, creativity, or anything else. No knowledge means no change, no reinforcement, no growth.

Truly, the incentives of pay and reprieve from one class induce many teachers to seek TT status. But few of them have the know-how to do their job. There is no graduate course in how to teach and evaluate ST's. Even if one were offered, it is doubtful that there would be sufficient demand to carry it. Even though colleges and school districts might offer such freebies courses, most prospective TT's wouldn't have the time and energy to attend.

Perhaps financial remuneration is not the only avenue to better classroom supervision although it appears to be most appealing to most people. Many CTP-CS's struggle valiantly to reward TT's in other ways—intellectually or psychologically: with offers of assistance in smoothing the graduate school road or at least warnings of booby traps to avoid; with letters of introduction or recommendation; with sympathy, advice, and good-natured bantering. Their purpose is to build a sense of obligation in TT's toward their ST's.

Most CTP-CS's are conscientious about their work. They visit their ST's classrooms many times in order to see many different situations, techniques, functions, good and bad. The more a CTP-CS gets to know

114

his ST's, especially as a result of weekly seminars, the more supportive he can be. At the same time, a CTP-CS must refrain from putting his unique stamp, his style on his ST's. He sees many classrooms in a number of schools and knows what is really happening, more so than anyone else on the team—P, TT, or ST.

There may be one more factor, the last piece, which has fallen to the floor and perhaps even disappeared under the rug, to make the picture incomplete. The final number, which is really the first, is the high school student.

Students' perceptions of ST's vary. Some find a young, vibrant, different teacher a delightful change. Others, who have a good image of their regular teacher, resent the usurpation by ST and become hostile. Still others see him as similar to a substitute, someone with whom they can get away with murder, take longer to settle down with. If he appears in body-shirt and flares, they see him as groovy and relate to him quickly. But if he only attempts to meet them halfway, perhaps through jargon or jokes but without really feeling or being with it, they quickly put him down.

Besides the physical picture the ST projects, there is the aura of the college man about him. If students see him as a representative of the college they are enamoured of or just as a college-student figure in general, they may turn on, curious about learning firsthand what college is really like. But on the other side of the tracks, the college image is a distinct disadvantage in a disadvantaged area:

> *What's this wise guy from Whitey's school doing here?*
>
> *What does he know about us—besides nothing?*

In a ninety-nine percent chancy situation, walled in by CTP-CS, TT, and P, ST may find that the student dimension may fall in on or out from under him too. Same old verse: creative teachers are born losers— before entering the profession, during the agonizing years of keeping their divergency and the system's convergency in balance, and after they have been squeezed out. From P's point of view:

> *So how does any P feel about teacher training? Like me, nothing, nothing. I let—take care of it.*
>
> *I'm too busy to waste my time chatting with some egghead CTP-CS.*
>
> *And there's nothing an absent-minded prof can tell me about administrating.*

*But I can bend his ear about that
long-haired hippie-type who's giving
___, my most reliable TT, a bad
time.*

*And his other goddam ST's have the
gall to park in the teachers' lot. They
belong in the street.*

And from CTP-CS's corner:

*God! I admire ST's' guts under the
barrage—kids, TT, and me.*

*I never thought ST would make it
with that veteran. But he really won
her over. What an operator!*

*It's amazing that his anxiety isn't
more visible. Of course, he does zig
when he should zag. But he's here to
learn, and I'm here to help him do
that.*

*And even the teachers in the lounge
are happy to see me. Of course, they
only want to know what course to
take next semester.*

*No one knows it better than
I—ST—standing before these
adolescents—sometimes lords of the
flies, sometimes stimulating curiosities,
sometimes just playful monsters.*

I stand here alone—I said

ALONE,

*baby. I mean, alone like that name on
a tombstone, like that mewling,
puking thing in the crib.*

Not alone. Remember the guy-gal
before you last semester?

And can I do my own thing?

Your own thing, if I don't hear about
it.

*Wellll-yes, if that TT—sometimes
beauty, sometimes bastard, sitting in*

116

*the rear of the room writing,
writing—what, what?*

*Sometimes not even concerned—only
correcting, correcting.*

Should I choose this word or that?

*Is he a swinger, that one in the back
seat, or a square?*

*And those kids, them and their eyes,
their nonchalance:*

*"I dare ya, man, Turn me on, like pot
or acid or uppers."*

*"Turn me on with your words, your
actions, your crap."*

> *Keep them under control, no matter
> what.*

*So they're all on me—that veteran
teacher who thinks, knows he can do
it better, faster, with fewer words, and
more efficiently*

But I can't do his thing, in his style.

*And they hate me, those kids, from
the word go.*

*Hate today but love tomorrow. And
hold no grudges.*

> *Authority.*
>
> *Parent Figure.*
>
> *The head, the boss, the putter downer.*
>
> *The Phoney.*

*Prove you're not by what you accept
and share.*

> *Maybe I'm not seeing them clearly.
> Maybe that hostility is in me, not
> them.*
>
> *Of course, they can put me on like
> Wow. They're so good at caricaturing
> adults. And they'd sure use it against
> me if they could. But maybe only till
> they know me better, know me,
> anyway.*

117

But there they sit, waiting for my first
word, the one that makes or breaks
me.

No singer, actor ever had it so rough.
At least their audiences choose to
listen, to come, are not forced to walk
lock-step from cell to cell, day after
day, year after year, more put down,
put upon than turned on.

              I'm like that Broadway critic. One
              word from me and you're done for—for
              life.

Now who's that who just slipped in
the back door. My CTP-CS, I suppose.
Haven't met him yet.
God! He looks stern.

What's that he's setting down on the
desk. A tape recorder?
It's just my technique. How else can
you hear yourself?

              Oh, no! How can I defend myself
              against that abomination—the
              damning evidence from my own
              mouth to make into interaction
              matrices, screw me to the
              behavioral-objectives rack.

I'd videotape if I could.

              Now I have three masters to serve.

              Where do I, oh creative soul, come in?

              Are they still there—the students, I
              mean?

                      They're captive, remember?

              Perhaps if I close my eyes at least one
              of them will go away—the kids, CS, or
              TT.

              What? Did the door open again?
              Ferchrissake! I think it must be P.
              And he brought—who? The
              department chairman?

              I'm out of my skull. It's more than I
              can take.

*I'm leaving this God-forsaken room
for a short break "on the grass."*

> *You can't leave. Remember: teachers
> have no "breaks."*

*Did someone ask a question? Which
one? Where did that voice come from?*

*In front of me? Behind me? In the left
corner? The right?*

Oh, oh! I'm afraid to look up!

*If I could wish them all away, who'd
be left?*

*When you and they are right on,
they'll all be gone but you and the
kids.*

> *I want to be creative, but every time I
> get an idea and think of that lesson
> plan—number one, that is, which must
> satisfy TT, and number two, which I
> write for CTP-CS, there isn't much
> left of me to put down on the one I
> teach from.*

> *And then, when I use that, sometimes
> the kids turn me off.*

> > *Just turn in those reports. They tell
> > me all I want to know.*

> *Where, oh where am I?
> I wish there were someone I could
> talk to about all this.*

> *How about an executive committee of
> kids? Maybe they could help me out.
> Like the blind leading the blind.*

Try it! They'll like it!

> *My TT is so busy most of the time.
> And I wish I could say that what he's
> doing isn't important. But I can't.*

> *My CTP-CS is available twice a week.
> But since he's evaluating me, I
> wonder if he'll think it's a sign of
> weakness or incompetency if I ask for
> advice.*

119

When was honesty ever a weakness?

> *No use trying P or the department*
> *chairman. Even TT can't find them.*

> > *I've got all those records to keep,*
> > *reports to write, hassles to squelch.*
> > *Sorry. No time for you.*

Now those buddies of mine in that
one seminar I have are pretty good
about giving me tips, especially when
CTP-CS listens to each of us letting
our hair down.

That CTP-CS last semester didn't do
anything but give us more of the
same—methods, corny philosophy from
twenty years ago.

There's some good in everything.

And here I am—sitting-duck—
surrounded by all of them on all
sides: if not by hostility or I-dare-you
or do-it-as-well-as-I-can, baby or let's-
uphold-the-standards-of-our-college.

All the while trying to create on my
own, pausing before every word,
syllable even, for fear it will bring the
wrong reaction from one of them at
the wrong time.

Will someone please call my Mom?

Momma, where's Poppa?

I'm Momma.   *I'm Poppa.*

.... **End Reflections**

120

Part II

Other CT's—Undone

Too bad
    For you.
        But more than you,
            Those kids
                Whom you turned on

                    Burned you
                Too,
           So that
        You
      Turned
      For
      Survival
      Down
      Other
      Paths,
         Away from
            Those you
               Care for,
                  Share with,

And others
        Turned off,
                While you stood by
                            To
                            Witness
                            The
                            Decimation
                            And
                            Cremation
                            Of
                    Creativity.
            And the fire
Caught and

Whose hands
        You clasp
                Are
                    Wrested
                        From
                        You.

Chapter 10

The Screwing of the First Year

Most first-year teachers get screwed—by the system, their superiors, and/or their more experienced colleagues. The mortality rate is extraordinarily high. Very often the most eager, idealistic, and creative are so shafted that they flee the profession forever—total dropouts.

FLASH!
40% URBAN TEACHERS LEAVE DISTRICT FIRST YEAR

Some remain, hiding behind a one-way glass that cuts them off from students' penetrating eyes. But young people recognize the expeditious surrender to the system made by the authority figure behind the desk. Still other teachers assault the students, taking out their own guilt and remorse on the forced inmates, who cannot understand why they have to knuckle under.

Don't ask so damn many questions!

What did I do this time?

The neophyte teacher does not often walk through the portals of his first public school into a climate of creativity. Usually the noncreative pattern has already been set. Often more than two thousand students are spread throughout buildings fiendishly designed by archi-

125

tects whose only awakening will come when they are obliged to live a year in their abominations. Everybody is his superior: principals, vice-principals, or assistant deans of boys and girls (not students), admissions and attendance officers, counselors, sometimes-officious clerical help, and finally the perceived owners of the establishment, the bus drivers and custodians.

Their fellow teachers—some of them only a year removed from the college they both shared, who might be helpful and not join in on the rat-packing, are hardly waiting eagerly to welcome their compatriots, to accept and share:

> *Well, here comes another one, puffed*
> *up with idealism. Wait'll he hits the*
> *stone wall. He'll change fast enough*
> *and become one of us. Let him learn*
> *the hard way, the way we did.*

Others, in the years they have spent there, did not have the sense to smell the pollution nor the guts to get the hell out of there before they were infected by the debilitating Chinese water torture:

d
r
i
p
no change

d
r
i
p
no encouragement

d
r
i
p
no reward

Most of them have had it, their creative efforts squashed at every turn:

How about it?

> *Maybe.*

Any decision yet?

126

We'll see.

May I?

          No.

Reflections..

You think this is crap? Exaggeration? Fantasy? Try it on for size, baby. And why aren't *you* in some classroom?

Nobody, it seems, accepts him for what he really is—a new teacher with many adjustments to make. It appears that the top administrator and his cohorts have forgotten their own first harried days of apprenticeship. They share no knowledge or experience with him. They aren't about to stop around to chat, to help him with problems, to encourage his own plans. No real acceptance, no true sharing, and certainly no stimulation.

Little chance that teachers either are open and accepting or have anything constructive to share. The greatest consolation they can offer is six survival commandments:

<table>
<tr><td align="center">Thou shalt:</td><td align="center">Thou shalt not:</td></tr>
<tr><td>I. Get with the system
as soon as possible</td><td>I. Make any waves</td></tr>
<tr><td>II. Keep the kids quiet
in the classroom</td><td>II. Ruffle the principal's
secretary</td></tr>
<tr><td>III. Join the right
organization</td><td>III. To thine ownself be true</td></tr>
</table>

..........................**End Reflections**

Deluged! From the moment he enters the main office, he's overwhelmed with paper. Someone once remarked:

> *The end of the educational world will be neither by fire or flood but by suffocation with dittoed material, memoranda, communiques, or orders from headquarters.*

Enter CT.

WOW! Three hours for orientation!
People and papers. Papers and
people. I can't tell one of those faces
from another.

*Which one did they say was the dean
of girls and which the dean of
boys—the one with the long hair or
the one in the pantsuit?*

*Who do my kids go to? The odd
counselors or the even?*

*What does the registrar do that an
attendance clerk can't?*

*Why in the hell do just teachers have
to wear name tags?*

*And those forms! The pink, the
yellow, the blue, the magenta, the
shit-colored one. Wilder than my last
trip!*

Reflections.......................................

Remember? The principal is primarily a papers person, not a people person.

Maybe there is a "new teacher orientation" and maybe there isn't—a preopening lecture to acquaint new teachers with forms, procedures, resources, and the myriad details that all institutions seem to become strangled by.

If there is no orientation, which is very often the case, he goes it alone—stumbling and bumbling, crawling to other teachers and begging for assistance. If he misses or does it wrong, his erstwhile compatriots chew him out.

Each educational system has its own attendance procedures and house rules about class cuts, tardies, and suspensions. Then come special testing periods, progress reports, fund-raising drives. When a teacher's thing is helping kids do their things, he usually balks at the waste of time and energy spent in red-tape–type activities. He defects. He joins the hypocritical generation. He puts first things first, our CT, and that's kids.

.... End Reflections

Our unsuspecting CT marches down the corridor laden with demands, requests, and orders. If he happens to encounter a sympathetic student, he may be directed quickly to his room, his very own first classroom—a box of course, a replica of the uncreative environment he has endured and survived somehow. Quickly he surveys the space:

I seem to have seen this place before,
about seventeen years worth. Funny.
Looks the same from this side of the
desk. A pukey green box.

I'll be damned if my kids will suffer
the way I did! Where are those
photos? Have I any posters? Ah, here.

Now what? No bulletin boards,
ferchrissake? Zap! Wood walls.

Hammer. Thumb tacks. Groovy!

Now, where can I put my books? No
bookcases either? Well, the window
sill will do, I suppose.

Maybe I can arrange my reading
corner over there—if I can move
twenty desks out of here.

Reflections..

That box-shaped room is what he has dreamed of for years. But in old rural or inner-city schools, the classroom *per se* usually consists of three solid walls painted barf green and one filled with windows. It is high-ceilinged, ill-lighted, and furnished with splinter-ridden, carved-up, tablet-arm lecture seats. Perhaps a glass- or wood-doored cabinet; a tattered flag; and dented, moldy wastebaskets complete the decor. He may eventually liberate bookcases and file cabinets. But not tonight, baby.

And so he settles down, boxed in and cut off from life—for life.

.... **End Reflections**

No matter what else is there, the kids always manage to turn the place on. With those kids figuratively on his shoulder, he begins to rearrange, revamp, revitalize his lesson plans.

When can I show those slides I
brought back from Canada? Let's see.
Just before Thanksgiving, about
War-of-1812 time?

Where do I order that slide projector
from? Who was it the principal said I
had to send an order to, and how far

129

*in advance? And did he say we had a
slide projector? Or was that a movie
projector he was talking about?*

*At State we had some great films. I
wonder if I can get any of those here?*

*Good grief! All the films for the year
have been ordered. I won't be able to
put my order in until spring—for
next year.*

*Let's see the list. Gee! I don't think
any of these apply to my subjects. And
so old! Screw them!*

*My poor kids will have to go
movieless or be bored. Maybe by that
time I won't care either. About their
being bored, I mean.*

*And when the kids get here, will I
have time for them? Ordering
projectors, filling out forms, checking
out texts. WOW!*

*If I only had one more free period for
doing this jazz before all the staff
goes home at 3:30 and I can't get into
those textbook, supply, and equipment
rooms. They never gave me keys for
them.*

I don't even have a key for the john!

Reflections.......................................

In college his audio-visual instructor had insisted that he learn how
to use all the latest machinery available to teachers to produce and
reproduce visual and auditory teaching aids. So he did.

But he soon finds that he can't duplicate diagrams, transcribe among
media, or even run the pre–World War II movie projector. Most schools
have too few such antiques; sometimes have screens, record or tape
players; and certainly more than enough obsolete textbooks and allied
materials. But a new teacher may lesson-plan a crackerjack unit only
to find that films are unusable or missing; overhead projectors nonexistent; THE matching texts all checked out by department colleagues; and transparencies, blank audio tape, workbooks, and even
staplers and ditto paper overdue—from last year's supply order.

130

Administrators usually fill orders only to the amount currently needed, not enough to supply new teachers added to expanded or new departments. Then again, other schools require teachers to order equipment themselves from a central, downtown office. Catalogs are notoriously incomplete or missing all together. The equipment itself is often in disrepair and its unreliable temperament unforgettable.

.... **End Reflections**

Do I supply them with paper and pencils if they come unprepared? No one mentioned THAT at the meeting. Maybe they don't want to admit they have any poverty-stricken kids. Well, have I got news for them! In my student teaching experience . . .

I bet they won't have, or won't bring or won't remember pencil and paper. Even if they start out with them, they'll have lost the pencil by fourth period. Well, I'd better buy some and have envelopes to keep them in here in the room.

Maybe I can scratch around in wastebaskets for misprinted ditto and mimeo paper they can use the backs of. I'll bet the administration doesn't even think of saving it. No room to store it anyway.

How come they don't think about us teachers once in a while and how it really is in the classroom?

Reflections......................................

Few businesses could survive if they used such haphazard procedures and jerry-rigged equipment. They do not ask their employees to provide their own special tools and machinery. Many teachers spend an average of two hundred dollars a school year on preprinted ditto masters, supplemental paperback books, and specialized equipment necessary for their subject, not to mention the time and energy expended to find them.

To a new teacher, knowing who and where to go for what may be the biggest hurdle he surmounts in the first year. The principal may

131

even mark him down on his evaluation for not using multimedia learning. At the same time P is too often not around when our CT is desperate to know the who's, where's, and when's of anything.

.... End Reflections

Swamped, inundated by papers from the paper-people, he glances at his program for solace. He knows that classes are labeled A for accelerated, bright, or gifted; B for above average but not quite shiny bright; C for the really average, the mediocre, the middle of the IQ range or a little lower; X, Y, Z for the hopeless ones; the discontented, turned off, emotional and intellectual failures clearly labeled D or F.

At this point he remembers that the principal promised him two average classes, one advanced and two slow, all within one grade level.

What lot did I draw? First period, C group; second period, X; third period Y; fourth period, Z. Oh no! It can't be true. What about sixth? Thank God. Another C.

Cool it a minute, baby. What grade level? ALL FOUR?

What the blazes is going on here? A math class the second period? I can't even add two and two. And history? OK. But what about all that reading I'll have to do?

Well, I'll do my best with what I have. Just wish I had at least one above-average class. How many years will I have to wait?

All right. Sock it to me. I said, 'I'd teach,' without reservations.

After all, kids is kids. Bright or dull, black or white, turned on or off.

Reflections ....

It is usually true that first-year teachers get their deepest shafting by the program. All the leftover students and subjects get tossed together and dumped into new teachers' laps. Often they have a class or two in areas they aren't qualified for: math-music or home economics-P.E.-science or history-ceramics-typing. They also may have to prepare for the whole grade range of the school, as many as six levels in combined junior and senior high schools.

As if these two dimensions weren't enough, the third one really queers it. Euphemistically called ability grouping, usually denounced as rigid tracking, but actually based on group IQ scores from the dim elementary school past, students are divided into fast, average, and slow groups. Even veteran CT's have misgivings about their effectiveness with the lower groups. But most veterans, CT or no, have earned the right to C, B, and sometimes A classes. At most, their programs include only one slow group. However, this standard may not hold for some schools which have predominantly a minority, poor, or otherwise deprived clientele. In such schools there may not even be enough students for a fast group.

As most of the literature shows, these schools are most likely to have a preponderance of new teachers who, as soon as they can show enough scars and staying power, move on to greener—nay, whiter pastures. Therefore, most new teachers have most of the low classes at a time when they are least knowledgeable and practiced in coping with these young adults whose culture differs from that of the national majority.

His anxiety increases. He wishes he could confide in the older teacher standing before the neighboring classroom and looking formidable and secure. But he might be a particular friend of the principal, a golf or poker buddy. Later he encounters another babe-in-the-woods, and they console each other. It happened to him as well—the shaft, the screwing, but good.

.... **End Reflections**

More put-down to come: the first faculty meeting.

You want I should sponsor a club?
What kind? Any old kind? Hell, I've
never been a joiner myself.

Oh, everyone's expected to, huh? Who
says? Oh, the principal.

Well now, let me see. Stamps? Skis?
Sewing? Red Cross? Key Club? Future
Lawyers?

The principal emphasizes co-curricular clubs to meet the students' demands, and one club has not yet found a sponsor. He also mentions the fact that club sponsorship is considered in teachers' evaluations. His gaze roams, pauses momentarily on our CT.

133

Reflections ....

You wanna bet?

.... **End Reflections**

Our hero ends up with a club he has no particular interest in or aptitude for. He is torn between wanting to do everything he can for his students yet is saddled with all those preparations. Overhanging it all, the threat of an evaluation.

And sponsor of one of the classes as
well? I guess the sophomores can do
the least damage, and demand the
least. Oh, someone has that one. Well,
does he need an assistant?

Sir, I'd like to sponsor . . .

You take this one.

Reflections ....

Alternatives? Whose?

.... **End Reflections**

The department meeting—no, departmentS' meetings next. Since he is teaching in more than one subject area, he feels compelled to attend them all. His major department is choosing a new book for the second semester. Another member of the hierarchy, the chairman, glances in his direction. He is the only new department member, so his head moves in only one direction—up and down:

Aye, aye, sir.

Another job. His thoughts move frantically farther and farther away from his original commitment to those kids in his classroom: first the club, now a committee to choose a text.

When do I teach?

Reflections ....

The day-to-day working conditions for teachers have not improved greatly over the years. Yes, there may be noon aides for playground

134

and hall supervision during certain times of the day. But teachers are also assigned to the same duties. Yes, there may be a security guard, but in times of real stress the male P.E. teachers are often told to perform riot squad duty. Interest, activity, and class groups multiply and need teacher sponsorship. Teachers are expected to supply recommendations for library purchases, to phone and visit students' homes, to attend in-service training, meetings, and special events—all of these often on their own time and without remuneration.

These procedures are usually the same for veterans and neophytes, but at least the veteran has some self-devised, automated systems to take much of the labor out of detail work. But with no back-up systems of surefire lessons, exciting materials, and procedural know-how, the neophyte finds extra duties very demanding. He has to know and do everything all at once—like yesterday.

However, there are those veterans, who generally avoid as many duties as they can and bitch about the ones they must perform. The goof-offs always make it harder for the movers, and hardest for neophytes, who want to be part of the action if only someone will tell them where, when, who, and how it is.

.... **End Reflections**

They mean well. They expect him to feel at home, one of the gang, a member of the teachers' (and administrators') organization.

Come to the next meeting.

He pays his dues although he wasn't asked whether or not he wanted to join.

It's expected.

How in the hell do I know which one of the three I want to be a part of? I didn't even know their names before they mentioned them.

Here we go again. The principal favors this one. So what does that make me? That one is considered radical, opposed to the school board. And the third one, the independent. Only kooks join that one.

I can't afford to join all three. In fact, not one, but . . . What the hell kind of choice is that?

135

Sign me up. I'll go the principal's
route. Wish I could get acquainted
first. Oh, well. Fly now. Pay—through
the nose—later.

He leaves the meeting with mixed feelings. He enjoyed the camaraderie. All the neophytes were there, but he knew he should have said no when they pressed him to be on that salary committee. He has special talents they might use; but his creative feelings, so strong the first morning he entered the school, seem to be ebbing away, drained by so many activities not directly related to his students' welfare nor his real interest in teaching.

Reflections..

There was a time when principals vied to be the first school to get all their staff members to join the local professional group, which also allowed him membership as well as his teachers. Nowadays, there are campus-wide, city-wide, state, and national groups. Nowadays, there are strikers, activists, reactionaries, and special interest groups to provide many alternatives, and principals have read the message.

All organizations zero in on him. CT wants a piece—but of which action? He may walk out, union member or not, for a day or a month. Or he may try to find out which way most of his colleagues are headed and follow them. He may opt for an interest group, where the politics are less heated, or a small crowd which plays at sociability. Hopefully, he may eventually discover one which treats him as a human being, a teacher, and creative.

.... **End Reflections**

How he struggles through that first semester he never knows. In fact, there are times when he feels like leaving to take a job in industry, especially when his best friend and colleague leaves in the middle of the term because of his frustration. Maybe he can get a job with him during the summer. And it might work into something permanent. Oh, he'd miss the kids, especially that second period class, that so-called "low" group he'd dreaded to meet at first. But they turned out to be a pretty good gang. Imagine those creeps giving him an end-of-the-year present, as though they sensed his uncommitted feelings. He never could really tell about young people. He'd learned that much at least, and he felt good about it.

136

There are those long days that now lie behind him when he could have used some suggestions. He had tried a few creative ideas. But the film which he expected would generate gut-level discussion had bombed out. The art masterpieces he had brought to broaden their world had elicited only snickers and wisecracks about the naked broads. He had expected them to listen with rapt admiration to the beautiful tones of a famous actress. With her first emotional utterance they had screamed with embarrassed laughter.

He would have liked to discuss these disasters with someone. He should have made an appointment with the supervisor, but there were those trips with the club members, the faculty meetings, the committee meetings. And he still had to check on those textbooks. There was the course he was taking at the university. And his wife's pregnancy hadn't been going so well.

Reflections..

Married	*Unmarried*
What kinds of social activities are there for my wife and me?	Where are the swingers? Who are they?
Is there a co-op nursery school? My wife's got to work, at least this first year, until I finish my masters.	A ski club? You better believe I do!

Other professions seem to have time to enjoy conviviality in mixed groups of doctors, lawyers, and businessmen and also in their own interest groups. Teachers seldom have time for more than a smile, nod, or "How are you?" to their colleagues as they rush past each other in the hall. Yet administrators do not plan activities to bring like-minded teachers from various departments within social communication range. If a neophyte wants to make friends in a community, he's got to do it on his own, sans principalis.

Many neophytes continue their education because additional credits and degrees mean salary increments over and above seniority advancement. But while they're about it, the seductive appeal of a staff position or a higher rung on the line ladder, coupled with the creativity-crippling frustrations of too much of everything too fast, may conspire to drive them into that list of next year's teacher dropouts.

.... **End Reflections**

So he lies there, exhausted, wondering whether he has the courage to start it all over again next year—especially after a strenuous summer session at the local teachers' college.

It must all add up to something for him. He has learned, of course. But what? Maybe how to avoid being screwed next time. He has almost become acquainted with the adolescents who passed through his classroom, often too quickly, as he rustled papers and wrestled with the inevitable forms he has finally become adept at completing. With the help of other creative neophytes he has succeeded in scratching the surface of the system, but their marks seem carved in sand. They have not really even dented the rock of the larger, more entrenched aspects of the system which continues to rule them.

And the kids he had hoped to stimulate. What of them? He wonders whether they really felt his presence—then, now, or ever. To some he may have been merely another authoritarian figure—an old man, an old maid, to be dismissed as they left his classroom in June.

This CT returned, determined that some day at least the kids would know he accepted them, shared with them, and, hopefully, stimulated them. Screwed he had been. But screwed he would not remain.

138

Chapter 11

Bugged Again

Reflections.......................................

The biology (or "bugs") teacher in the secondary school examines with his students that greatest of man's creations—the BODY. For the adolescent just discovering his, it's a fabulous experience. But for the CT it is both a joy and a threat. The students' curiosity assures the instructor of at least 75% undivided attention. However, on some day at some hour a conscientious biology instructor, resplendent in the lab coat, must discuss, bring up, or admit to the problems and pleasures of SEX, at least its physiological implications.

The writing or lecturing scientist is immune to attack by moralists. But the same protection does not exist for the teacher-scientist in the classroom. An experienced teacher may bird-and-bee the issue with expertise. He deludes at least some of his students into thinking that they are learning a great deal about the mystery of mysteries. The more naive teacher, however, may blunder into offending the community with the best of intentions.

.... **End Reflections**

An imaginative, trusting health teacher leveled with his students. Together they developed considerable rapport. And as part of the required course of study he strove to enlighten them about the ways humans relate sexually. He brought into the lab embryos from his neighborhood butcher shop. He showed the "Oregon" films. He moderated a panel of two doctors—one male, one female—who responded frankly to students' questions.

As their knowledge grew, he also tried to correct any misinformation they might have learned from their friends. He distributed a dittoed list of often misunderstood terms about sex, along with their translations into scientific terms. He felt secure within the four dismal walls of the scientific laboratory, confident in the mutual trust he and the students had built. But almost within the hour he learned about the foolhardiness of his action.

A girl, his most devoted student, innocently showed the list to her parents.

How was CT to know that her father was president of the school board?

Chapter 12

Bearding the Bearded

| 196?: Friday the 13th: | Teachers' meeting before opening |
| 8:30 A.M.: | of school. (CT displays summer beard to buddies.) |

8:31 A.M.: Principal warns CT: no beard on Monday, the first day of classes.

I was warned about this guy. I'd better call the Superintendent right away.

I was warned about this guy. I'd better call my union rep.

Monday the 16th: School opens.

8:30 A.M.: CT meets P in hall. P says go.

8:31 A.M.: CT goes.

That was too easy. Miss ____, make an appointment for me at the Superintendent's office.

That was too easy. What bar was I supposed to meet those guys at?

Wednesday the 18th:	CT in Superintendent's office.
10:00 A.M.	Given twenty-four hours to shave.
Thursday the 19th:	CT does not shave. P orders him
9:00 A.M.	to stay off campus.

*They told me this would be a long
case. How long can I hold out?*

*Is the district really prepared to go
through a long trial?*

How long will the union support me?

| Friday the 20th: | CT transferred out of high school |
| 10:00 A.M. | to home teaching position. |

*Thank God that hair is out of my
hair.*

*Can I survive outside of the
classroom? Oh, well. Kids are kids,
one at a time or thirty.*

196? + 1 year: Monday the 22nd: Court case opens.
                10.00 A.M.

196? + 3 yrs.: Thursday the 3rd: CT wins.
                3:00 P.M.

                Friday the 4th: CT files bankruptcy.
                1:00 P.M.

196? + 4 yrs.: Tuesday the 9th: CT back in classroom
                9:00 A.M.

196? + 6 yrs.: Friday the 12th: CT (still with beard) becomes
                2:00 P.M. member of administrative staff
which originally transferred,
prosecuted, and castigated him.
The grant he applied for and
received ($75,000) made him
"one of them."

Students, colleagues, and administrators remembered what he was
like before his beard had denied him to them:

*"He was one of the finest and most
interesting teachers I've ever had."*

*"He's one of the strongest teachers in
the system."*

142

*To deprive high school students of the
benefits of learning under one of the
most stimulating and inspiring
teachers in the school just because an
administrator has been brainwashed
by safety-razor advertising is a signal
of inept leadership and Babbitt-like
insistence upon conformity at any
price.*

> *He opposed the traditional plan of
> student government and caused
> trouble by urging students to
> challenge it.*

> *Who sets the policy—the schools or an
> individual union member? It's as
> simple as that.*

Reflections.......................................

From superior CT to excellent home teacher to efficient and innovative
administrator in eight years. That is the story of the Bearded One.
Mostly we are concerned with the events that led to such a rapid fall
and slow return. And the question we must reiterate: how much of
this sort of harassment can any CT take? What happens to the inner
fires of those CT's who are not so bold as to lay it all on the line
but who simply slip quietly just below the surface?

.... **End Reflections**

He was sought after:

*I haven't made up my mind about
leaving these boondocks for the big
city.*

> *It will be quite a change—from red
> desert to the concrete camp.*

> *Your experience with
> Spanish-American students impresses
> us greatly.*

They're just kids, like any others.

> *Your know-how and sensitivity would
> be invaluable in helping our teachers*

143

*understand culturally different
students.*

*Culture, shmulture. Students are
students the world over.*

Recruited from a neighboring state, where he had earned a Master's degree, taught for several years and was well respected by administrators, colleagues, and students alike, he was as successful in his new position at a ghetto junior high or off-campus as he had been in adobe brick.

*I learn more from him than from any
other teacher I've ever had.*

He gives the best parties in town.

When an opening developed for a teacher of American history at a WASPish, academically oriented senior high school across town, both parents and former students pushed for his appointment. He moved right in, and his reputation as a CT continued to grow:

*I gotta get in his class. My buddy
says he's the greatest.*

*I never saw so many kids so eager to
listen, to learn, for a whole period.*

He swings, man.

And swing he did—360 degrees worth. He went above and beyond the 180-degree classroom commitment and incited to change within his local professional organization in hopes of bringing about statewide changes—teachers running their own affairs:

*We've got to get more teachers on the
standing committees. All the key
offices are held by administrators.*

*If we don't get a majority of our boys
on the nominating committee, we
won't have a seat to sit on.*

*What do they mean—TEACHERS
Association. It's more like School
Managers Association!*

Reflections.......................................

Just as CT's beard formed shadowy first, then in vague outline, then all scraggly, then trimmed to neatness, and finally blooming in boldness,

144

so went his career. Both students and fellow teachers contributed to his growth, inner and outer, while P clipped and mutilated all the while.

.... **End Reflections**

The *shadow* on the wall: administrative and classroom:

> *What dynamics will operate now that he's on campus? I accepted him on P's recommendations from the junior high. But how will he be with eleventh and twelfth graders?*
>
> *Can he really prepare our elite for college? If he can't, what do I do?*
>
> *Well, there's the hot line to downtown. And I think I can trust the Superintendent.*
>
> *Even if this is my first year here, too, I've known all the downtown people for years.*

WOW! These kids are too much. Different from junior high. Movable. On wheels.

Where can we go? In town? Out of town?

And I can sure move their minds. We'll work through all the establishment requirements—ACT, CAT, GRE questions.

A week or two later:

Some board rules are stupid. Teachers' organization throwaways in and out of school mailboxes, ferchrissake! $\Big\}$ U, as in union

> *Some dress codes are stupid. Shirttails in and out, ferchrissake!* $\Big\}$ S, as in students

> *And . . . ?* $\Big\}$ CT

You've tried others. Why not try us? $\Big\}$ U

> *How about getting together Friday?* $\Big\}$ CT

> *We've tried. Nobody listens.* $\Big\}$ S

145

Try writing. The hot breath of change \} CT
sounds better through the pen.

They didn't seem too interested. \} U

       They turned us down again. \} S

   Well, let's try again. \} CT

We demanded. The Board refused. \} U

      We demanded. P refused. \} S

   Compromise. Bargain. Give a little \} CT
   and get a little.

It worked! \}   US   \{ *It worked!*

Reflections..

The *vague outline* appears on the wall, administrative and classroom:

     Well, something's starting here, but
     the end isn't clear.

     I keep hearing about what the kids
     say. What do they mean, they couldn't
     talk about "that" in Mrs. ____'s class.

     And the counselors are going berserk,
     trying to dig up enough college
     catalogs for all his kids who think
     they can hack it in college, with good
     grades or not.

Well, something's starting here. Let's
see how I carry it on.

What institutions and procedures are
closest to us—geographically,
affectively, intellectually. Which ones
need examining?

Wonder how P will take to it?

          .... **End Reflections**

 A month later:

Those SOB's downtown are mumbling \}
about a recount. All pro-union people \} U
won.

> *That SOB downstairs won't allow*
> *anyone to recount the song girl*
> *ballots. Three blacks ran and not one*
> *a winner.* } S

And . . . ? } CT

Let's put it to the state boys. } U

> *Let's put it to the councils—student*
> *and parent advisory.* } S

I'm with you. } CT

Reflections.......................................

The *scraggliness* appears—on walls administrative and classroom:

> *Some days it's all too much. It all*
> *began so well—so white, so true, so*
> *blue—all those parents out there in*
> *the bleachers cheering their lungs out.*

> *Why couldn't it stay that way? Must*
> *we have a black cheerleader, a black*
> *drum major?*

> *I'm sure all that snooping that CT's*
> *classes are doing is going to get us*
> *into trouble. Somebody in City Hall*
> *even mentioned it at that dinner last*
> *week.*

> *And those rumblings in the loyal*
> *teachers' organization. A new*
> *organization? Only one ever survives.*
> *And which one?*

> *I'd better have some of the newer*
> *teachers in for a conference and set*
> *them straight.*

> *Or will that stir up a hornet's nest?*

Some days it's really too much.

They sure want me in on all the
union doings. Should I go along?
Wait till next year?

And the kids are into both the
black-white scene and the
phony-baloney student government
one. Can they handle them both?

147

What happens if someone gets in the
way? Me? P?

.... End Reflections

Two months later:

> *We want a column, views from both*
> *sides, about anything—Vietnam,*
> *pollution, prejudice—in the school*
> *paper. But our advisor won't let us.* ⎫ S

We want new blood at the top. But ⎱ U
nobody will run for the spot. ⎰

> *Me and my big mouth. Well, I may as*
> *well go all the way as long as I've*   ⎬ CT
> *come this far.*

Reflections......................................

The *outline much clearer* on the wall—administrative and classroom:

> *Whew! So other P's are facing the*
> *same thing—rebellious students,*
> *black-white confrontations, each or*
> *both against browns.*

> *I'm not sure about abolishing student*
> *newspapers for lack of funds. I'd*
> *better take a closer look at*
> *underground ones, too.*

> *Better get the staff together to plan*
> *strategies, defenses.*

> *I'm going to get in my three years*
> *before retirement some way, any way.*

I wonder how many of us are facing
the same thing—taking over local
leadership of the union.

Who'd have thought those kids would
expose our own staff member—the
advisor an avowed Bircher.
Dynamite! But who could stop them?
What guts!

P had to give in on equal faculty
meeting time for both teachers'

148

organizations, especially with the
teachers' committee just aching to ask
some embarrassing questions if he
didn't.

Right on! And head on—conference
with P coming up.

.... **End Reflections**

By the end of the year the die was cast; the lines were drawing fast,
cracks in the ground between P's office and CT's classroom. Messages
were misunderstood. Rumors were flying:

I hear CT wants to transfer.

> *I hear P has already requested his*
> *transfer.*
>
> *But the other P doesn't really want*
> *him.*
>
> > *I hear the students are petitioning*
> > *and thinking of picketing.*

Where's the spirit in this place?

> *Rah! Rah! Rah! Our team's together.*
>
> > *Get rid of that rabble rouser!*

Even if I could find my colleagues on
this campus, I'm not sure they'd speak
to me.

> > *Serves him right. Why didn't he stay*
> > *in OUR teacher organization?*
> >
> > *Tell him to keep his grimy paws off*
> > *the news staff.*

Is it patriotic to protest against the
war?

> *Must student government always be a*
> *sham?*
>
> > *I'm proud of the high academic*
> > *standards you teachers have*
> > *produced.*

The kids want to swing, but the walls
are too close in.

> > *Why should teachers care about*
> > *conditions inside the kids inside the*

149

classroom? They're paid to teach, not analyze.

Reflections..

In the good ol' summing-up time, P, Eastside:

Happy days are—or are they? CT's gone from this school, thank heavens, but what about the gang he left behind? Can I really handle them—now?

Even my old trusties ask: why don't we become more aggressive?

And is that rumor true? Bussing one hundred blacks here next year? How can we keep up our academic standards?

I'd like to go to that union conference down south. But give up a week's vacation? Ah, the cause!

We're really making headway: fifty members in three months. And that favorable judgment in court didn't hurt us.

I'd better check in with my new P before we leave for our holiday. And then—the mountains! The boys'll love it. I won't shave the whole time.

P, Westside:
One more meeting and I'd have thrown in the towel. Everything at once: bussing, blacks, bills—bull!

At least I don't have union problems here—yet. But I wonder if I should have agreed to take CT on my staff.

Always like to do a favor for a fellow P, but I may be asking for trouble.

Then came the Fall. Stop me if you heard this one.

.... **End Reflections**

And he sat beside the beds of the home students, who no doubt deserved and got his best efforts. He recalled with regret those groups of eager ones who sought his counsel or accepted his challenges. His sacrificial attempt to make himself grow through dedication to principle, using the instruments of student and professional organizations, shook down no walls, destroyed no festering poisons, did nothing but close him out of the chance to make changes.

And what of the two principals and the superintendent, all of whom were deeply involved in the case of the Beard? One P retired. The other moved to another district as a lesser wheel and soon afterward retired. The superintendent left the district to become the head man of a more urban one but was hit and run over by a bus-sing.

They could not, any of these three, really cope with the too-fast-changing world. Each had been away too long from his life blood—the students.

And CT returned to his classroom charges, whose transfusions of the new order had revived him long enough to do battle with the admini-forces and to win, legally and morally.

Reflections ....

But for all the dancing in the streets, someone has to pay the piper. This time one CT, after four years of trial-by-fire, survived. What of the others, those CT's who, despite courage, stamina, and economics, are defeated from without? Are they defeated also FROM WITHIN?

In the area of self-protection, teachers have little recourse in the event of transfer or dismissal. Standards for credentialing and accountability are established by state legislators, often on the shifting sands of pressure from powerful lobbies. When bureaucrats say "Jump!" teachers never ask why.

Why?

Well, there are slim chances of success in battling administrative decisions. Dues paid to a local group FOR TEACHERS ONLY can supply legal counsel IF a favorable outcome may set a precedent or IF the group has a collective-bargaining arrangement with the school district. Otherwise, a teacher must buy his own mouthpiece and PERHAPS receive some consultation from the group. And pity the poor probationary teacher. He need not even be shown cause for firing. Administrators own not only the mitt, bat, and ball but the ballpark too, and expertise in gamesmanship. Flanked by administrative ruling, backed by superiors, he meets the divergence force head on, hard hat and all.

151

But, hopefully, the old order changeth—yielding place to HAIR.

.... **End Reflections**

Chapter 13

Rally Not 'Round

[*Do I really want this classroom scene?*] It was reported that a student teacher, completely engrossed in a classroom activity and frantically searching for a pointer, grabbed the standard to which the American flag was attached and used it. Within the hour, so the story goes, he was standing before the superintendent of one of the largest school districts in the world.

The flag incident was only one of the difficulties our CT was to face over the years. Let it be to the credit of the school who chastised him that they gave him his first teaching position. Within a few weeks he had an excitement going in his classroom.

Why not interview a few members of the school board to get their reactions as to why the school bonds failed again?

We're taking a trip to Synanon next week to find out where alcohol and drugs lead some people to.

But he made one of the most tragic errors a creative teacher can make. Elated about the "excitements" in his classes, he went to the faculty lunch room with the heat of learning still coursing through

153

his veins, talking about happenings to his colleagues. [*This adult, peer-teaching scene is something else, like a bed of nails.*]

Would you believe that one of my
students persuaded the president of
the school board to come to class next
week? Would any of the rest of you
like to bring your classes?

We got a promise from the local
printer that he'd do up our class
newspaper. For free, yet!

He was soon cooled. With each telling of a new project,

Imagine. Four consuls are coming to
our mock U.N. Security Council
meeting!

or an exciting discussion;

If psychologists want to give drugs to
politicians to make them more
sensitive and aware, why can't
students have them?

—his peers, after a brief "Is that so?" went on to discuss their accustomed topics—fondues, discount-house sales, bunion operations, usually with the teachers to their right or just across the table. When he arrived home somewhat frustrated by the turn-off and analyzed the situation with his wife, also a student-teacher CT by virtue of her highly rated performance by her college supervisor and supervising classroom teacher, they decided it would be wiser to save the exhaltation for home consumption rather than the faculty lunch room. [*Maybe a change of scene—another school district.*]

Reflections...

CT might have been an offensive person physically or psychologically, but he was not. Even if he had been strange in appearance or manner, his colleagues still might have been interested in a productive learning situation, either from the point of view of trying something new themselves or from the fact that their student-family was being highly motivated, or even pride in "one of their own."

Perhaps the other teachers were ego-threatened. Their students sat immobile, inattentive, or disruptive in their classes. The teachers were powerless to arouse them. This upstart CT was trying to sabotage the

154

conditioning process. Perhaps after ten years of teaching would be a more valid time to put his creative powers to the test. By then he might have simmered down, his creativeness weakened.

As hypothesized here, creativity is possible in each individual, especially with professional teachers. So what had happened to those colleagues who faced him during the lunch hour? They might have been conditioned by uncreative instruction at the college and university level. Maybe a lack of encouragement during their early teaching years had stultified them. In either event, they now resorted to the traditional approach of read and recite in their classes and strongly resented any interloper who was a threat to their uncreative commitment. Perhaps a few years before they had made the attempt to exert this innate creativity in the form of an unorthodox approach to a learning procedure and had been criticized for having too noisy a class. The gospel according to administrators and non-flap-making teachers reads: Keep the kids quiet and in their seats and the principal will not only ignore you but reward you—by further ignoring you.

.... End Reflections

CT left that school district, at least away from those colleagues whose first concern seemed to be the protection of their own egos and not the expansion of the egos of their students.

In his new assignment CT found respite from envious looks and veiled cracks about his way-out programs. He was somewhat more encouraged because the new geographic location was surrounded by a freer, more swinging, urbanized community more heavily populated with professionals of many broad viewpoints. The change gave him an opportunity to reassess his position, to examine his image more carefully in the mirror of teacher reflections. He found solace in writing about "Open Classrooms and Inquiry Methods of Approaching Social Studies" and "More Community Involvement for Students." [*Maybe I belong in the writing scene,*]

The articles about his experiments were published in a journal that examines carefully any material submitted, usually accepting only that of already well-established, seasoned educators. This professional acceptance led him to plan to become more involved in the politics of the school scene, and he joined that teacher organization that fostered a more activist point of view. [*—or union scene,*]

The next few years were prosperous ones for CT. Avenues for his creativity opened, and he held office in the local teacher organization. He was involved with a branch of the nearby university as a consultant

155

and a director of workshops. As part of his school assignment he was asked to chair the reorganization of the social studies curriculum and to investigate new approaches to the teaching of disadvantaged youth. These commitments filled his life, for a time anyway. [*—or higher education, teacher-training scene.*]

His restless, swinging spirit also searched out new experiences closer to his teaching area of social studies. Off he sailed to spend three years abroad, becoming part Halliburton, part teacher. [*Hm-m-m. Lotsa scenes here. Filming, exchanges, staying, import-export business.*] He stopped off from time to time to bring his talents to foreign students of Asia, Africa, and Europe. Both he and his wife experienced the reality of other cultures. They lived in the deprived areas of India, the Sudan, and Bolivia. Their associations took them into the homes of teachers in each of these countries. Whatever street they walked down became the world they lived in and accepted, all the smells, the sounds, the sights. [*Maybe the free-school scene.*]

They returned enriched and refreshed, and CT made applications to several school districts. Returns were slow, and although he was interviewed, no positions were offered. For several months he waited, hoping to secure a job that would promise the greatest opportunity for creativity. But that chance never came, and he finally accepted the next best.

Considering the dearth of teachers at that time, this situation sounds unbelievable. Hadn't he proven himself? But even more incredible was the fact that at that same time superintendents and personnel directors were making expensive trips to the Midwest to hire "cheap" teachers, often not even credentialed or certificated. It was a bitter blow to him to know that less competent teachers were being assigned to classes of students to whom he might have brought the enrichment of three years abroad. [*Oh, no! The dropout scene?*]

Finally a principal accepted him, recognizing the type of contribution he might make to the students in his school.

> *No one else wants to work in this district, and I can't blame them—If you can keep the kids in their seats, you're hired.*
>
> *Whatever techniques you use, I'll stand behind you.*

His acceptance also encouraged him to begin his work on an advanced degree.

156

Reflections ....

He began as a maverick. The incident of the flag marked him as different—impulsive, perhaps. Nothing of this possible example of poor judgment, however, was ever recorded anywhere in the placement file kept by the university. Yet administrators seemed to regard him as "too different," too much of a risk.

In selecting his teachers, a principal often relies on more than the printed matter in the applicant's files. Some systems send a "tracer," a request for information above and beyond the recommendations submitted by training teachers and deposited in the applicant's file after he has left the university campus. This practice puts the applicant in double, and secretive, jeopardy. Usually the official recommendation from the university is responsible for the first placement of the applicant. It is a detailed evaluation of the student's performance in the classroom. If a principal utilizes only this source, he subscribes to the legitimate source of evaluation. If he uses the "tracer" from the school district in which the applicant fulfilled his student-teaching assignment, however, he may view the applicant in a different, often less favorable light. In this incident, CT may have received one evaluation that never mentioned the flag incident; were a "tracer" sent to the principal of the school where it occurred, however, the hiring administrator might react negatively and thereby establish a grapevine system that would jeopardize CT's opportunities for employment in any school district.

If a candidate is labeled a maverick or oddball, his chances for employment or further advancement, once he is employed, may be limited. Any educator indoctrinated in the principle of respect for individual differences might say, "More power to the odd one." This type of applicant would stand high on such a principal's list. The kind of individual our "States" culture most often reveres, however, is usually cast in the mold of conformity.

Suppose an administrator must choose between two teacher candidates, both equally qualified yet one with a record that hints of nonconformity. Granted that the modern, urban administrator is beset by overwhelmingly complex problems—integration, disadvantaged youth, school bond failures, we can sympathize to the degree that he will probably select that candidate more likely to be "the quiet one" than one who might compound his supervisory duties.

On the one hand, the educator wishes to encourage initiative and independence in the classroom. On the other, he is forced by budget cuts and unhappy citizens to assume more and more responsibilities for holding together a disintegrating system. At this juncture he might well view the creative one more as a threat than a source of assistance. What he fails to realize, as he retreats, is that the best defense is a strong offense.

Acceptance means risk-taking, but an accepted one is very often a sharing one who could well stimulate the rallying of forces for creativity. [*The final scene?*]

.... **End Reflections**

Well, it's been a scenic trip. Some slides are really beautiful, some pretty grim and some I can't even figure out.

It all adds up to—what? In fact, where do I fit into it—this kaleidoscope, or montage.

That's it! Collage! That's me on top, accepted by those rejected kids—who would believe they would, or that I would accept them—and sharing with and stimulating them.

The next layer down is the reading of everything about anything, writing about my experiences and plans and 'rithmeticking up those units for another credential, a Ph.D. even.

And below that, my work for professionalizing the profession through the organization.

And then the shop—selling all those wild things we picked up on our travels.

My God! What a long way 'round!

Chapter 14

Creativity and Punishment

Two history teachers occupied classrooms side by side; they lived worlds apart. Stepping into the room of the CT—history was like time-machining. The nondescript walls were alive with charts, maps, and models. In the neighboring classroom of NCT—history was adorned only with the dullness of the walls; nowhere was the sense of history, past or present, in evidence. Maps were tightly encased in their racks as though never unrolled, never displayed. Even the blackboards of room number two were virginally black.

CT—history was alive; he communicated with, accepted, stimulated his students to be aware of history always, yesterday and today, with a sense of responsibility for the history they would make tomorrow.

We are here today; tomorrow we are
history.

Of course you can build a fort with
ice cream sticks.

Examine this community; What can
you do to improve it, now—today?

NCT—history rarely moved away from his desk—half alive, half listening while his students read interminably from the textbook, page after page, hour after hour, day after day. With glazed eyes his charges watched the minute hand of the clock move them closer to that speck on its face which signaled their blessed release by the bell.

> *Can't you read louder so that all the class can hear? Rick is falling asleep back there.*
>
> *Tomorrow we'll read the entire Constitution. Then maybe you'll understand its importance in history.*

These contrasting patterns cast their shadows over the desert sands for the three years of these two teachers' probationary periods in this school district. Finally came the day of accounting—that hour when tenure would or would not be granted. Generally, many in that day were called, and in that day many were chosen. But not in the case of these two. Which of them, CT or NCT, would be retained?

Living next door to each other in the school, these two candidates seemed not to be on the same planet.

One moved in the community of political activity.

> The other stood in neutral territory, passive and inactive.

The one was a reader of political tracts, yesterday's and today's.

> The other read only the comics and the sports of the dailies.

One had fought in the frontlines.

> The other remained behind to train the young to kill.

The first lived in ranch country, the land of the free.

> The other chose the entombment of the suburbs.

The one treated students as humans.

> The other counted bodies in seats.

The one had a voice full of excitement, light- and dark-toned.

> The other droned on in a monotone.

One was absorbed in the world of his subject.

160

The other walked through and away
from even the text.

One moved in the circle of real men
and women.

The other associated only with the
flickering images on the TV screen.

To their students they said:

*Post those charts high. Everyone in
the class is interested in those
percentages of new arrivals to this
community.*

*Turn the page and read the first
paragraph on the next—louder!*

*Get out there and interview those
citizens. Then write up the reports for
our class newspaper.*

*Answer all the questions at the end of
the chapter and be sure they're
written in ink! Remember: neatness
counts.*

*I can't give all of you A's, but you
deserve them. I'm writing notes of
commendation to all of your parents.*

*Failure notices will be out tomorrow
and most of you will be getting
one—all except those who have been
able to be heard.*

*Think, you smart a-a-apples, and
keep thinking.*

*If you want to pass this course, you'd
better memorize those pages.*

And the students replied:

I can't wait to get out of his class.

I can't wait to get into his class.

Only the walls, dull or cluttered, heard the words. Only the walls
knew and the CT-excited and NCT-dulled students knew, and they
weren't listened to, nor did they speak up.

Reflections.......................................

161

The school administrators of this community had not established policies to evaluate accurately either of these teachers.

1. They did not visit either class, even when the more aggressive students complained about NCT.
2. They were also prone to listen to "grapevine" drippings rather than gather direct evidence.

They seemed not to be concerned with encouraging creativity in CT by:

1. Commending CT for the innovative projects he encouraged: the Rumor Clinic and the workroom he had set up for the less able student.
2. Asking him whether or not there was something they could do in assisting him to set up the model U.N. conference with other high schools in the district.

The supervisors did not stimulate creativity in NCT by:

1. Suggesting other methods to be used beyond the recitation technique, visual aids that might relieve the boredom.
2. Scheduling conferences with all teachers to get some feedback and make recommendations.
3. Sending him materials which might move him to consider other alternatives.

Administrators had, in both cases, neglected that most important facet of their official function: the improvement of instruction for the benefit of both student and teacher growth and development.

.... End Reflections

Both CT and NCT now stood before the board members, and a decision had to be made. Upon what could the members, as they looked at both of them and at each other, base their evaluations?

The members reflected on the one:

He's a stalwart member of the community. He goes to church each Sunday.
He makes no loud sounds in faculty meetings. He's raising a family
in one of the better suburbs of the community. He knows nice
people in the housing tract, plants his grass seed, drinks
a beer with his neighbor, puts up a swing set for his kids—
blonde towheads, both of them. His wife meets with
the faculty wives and does a good job when they

162

*have a money-raising drive. I've heard him
talk politics once or twice, and he seems
to agree with the status quo—a strict
constructionist. I remember he
once said he was in the
service—a flyer or
ground-school
trainer*

The other was hard to categorize:

*His wife
doesn't look like
the others, wears "funny"
clothes at times. Oh, she's a
good enough woman—took an orphan in
for a while. Still, she looks kind of
foreign, doesn't quite belong in the faculty
wives' group. I hear she makes great chili; I've
never tasted it. Isn't he running for some political
committee office? Which party is it, anyway? Oh, that one?
Well, where did he get that dark complexion? His kids, too. That
long black hair. Central America? At least, it isn't from JUST across
the border.*

Their teaching?

*My son's friends say he's kinda dull; but then, I had plenty of that kind
when I was in school, too. Didn't hurt me. Of course, we don't
want a complete loser. Still, his classes are quiet, or so they
say. He doesn't tolerate any nonsense, they say. I think
he's used a movie once or twice when someone else
ordered them. Have to give him a little credit.
After all, history isn't the most interesting
subject. He's always at the football
games. I've seen him there myself.
Sounds safe, doesn't he?*

*Your
daughter
says he's ex-
citing? How does
she mean that? Funny,
the kids don't seem to mind*

163

that dummy arm he's got. Wonder
how his wife . . . Of course, I didn't
like that Rumor Clinic thing, whatever
that was. The editor of the local newspaper
called me on that one, said he'd heard two teachers
had been shot. Don't think that kind of publicity helps
the school's image any. And that UN assembly, or whatever it
was. They're really against that down in the city. Maybe we ought to
be careful.

Well, we can't afford both of them. Which shall it be?

What's that you say? Some new evidence on the dark one? Notices sent out
without administrative approval? What kind? Oh, commendations? To all
the parents? Do any of the other teachers use that form? There
is no official form? And he didn't discuss it with anyone?
Sounds a little like insubordination. Do you think we can trust
him? If anything serious happens, I mean? That's the trouble
with those political activists. You never can tell. Well,
I've made up my mind. How about you? And you? OK.
Besides, he won't have any trouble getting a job
down in the city. They like that kind down
there. Well, let them have him. The
other might have a rough time get-
ting another job. I heard him
say once he'd like to try Driver
Ed. I sorta like those
quiet guys.

Reflections....................................

Many were called, but this time only one was taken—NCT.

The students and citizens lost on two counts. They retained an inadequate, uncreative instructor and lost a valuable CT and citizen.

.... **End Reflections**

CT reflected:

I just can't figure it out. Why? Why?
Where did I go wrong?

The best I can come up with is that I
sent those commendations home

*without going through channels and
miffed someone, somewhere along the
line.*

*Maybe it's because I worked for the
_____ Party. Hell, even some
administrators are in it. Not as
actively as I, however.*

*In fact, I hardly hear any of them
talk politics.*

*That reactionary editor sure wasn't
any help. How come he has such
influence around here?*

Do you suppose Upton Sinclair's The
Brass Check *is still well and living
here—now?*

Still . . .

Surely, his Latin American ancestry did not aid his case. They knew he had been related to one of the past presidents of a small, trying-to-emerge country. The president, of course, was a revolutionary one.

*And why all the anger and shouts
when I asked them to put their
criticisms in writing?*

> *We are not compelled to put anything
> in writing for probationary teachers!*

*Where in the hell can a teacher find
any protection?*

*Maybe I'd better think it again—about
joining the union, that is.*

*The family is sure going to miss the
wide open spaces. Maybe we can find
a little acreage "down there."*

*Hm-m-m. I wonder if my vets'
organization would plead my case. I
hate to drag up the Purple Heart bit.*

*Hell! They have no respect for my
mind. Why should they for my body.*

*Well, damn me and what's-his-
Russian-name—Raskolnikov.*

I didn't even commit a crime, and I'm punishing myself.

Screw 'em.

Chapter 15

Gettysburg—
One More Time

Committed, competent, creative. [". . . *a new nation* . . ."] He was all of these, a CT-English teacher, even before he entered his permanent classroom. Encouraged by an enterprising supervising teacher during his student-teaching experience, he devised an excellent scheme for illustrating writing style. [". . . *conceived in Liberty* . . ."] Combining a tape recording of Civil War songs with the narration of Lincoln's Gettysburg Address, he challenged his junior high students to examine that most elusive element—an author's style. What should happen, he proposed, if another person, especially an English teacher, were to tamper with the sentence patterns and word choices of such eloquence? [". . . *created equal* . . ."] His objectives were clearly defined; his rationale sound; and the ultimate execution of his plan, coupled with a creative response from his students, proved him correct.

All of his students knew of Lincoln's tremendous contribution to man's understanding of man. Many of them had committed the Address to memory in elementary school. An analysis of why the words, placed as they were, had had such a phenomenal effect on so many men of such different cultures was most appropriate to a study of language development.

He distributed dittoed copies of the selection to his students. The script had been slashed by the inevitable red pencil of an imagined,

unimaginative English teacher's correcting hand. ["... *so dedicated*..."]
He credited his source, *Mad Magazine,* a publication which had
particular relevance for his adolescent students. That a stodgy (short
hair), old (age twenty-five) English teacher would condescend not only
to read some of these students' favorite magazines but to reproduce
a copy for each of them made him acceptable, a swinger. The stage
was set. The enthusiasm grew. The effect was achieved.

Everyone hurrahed: the supervising teacher, the college supervisor,
the principal, the kids. [". . . *have consecrated it* . . ."] CT had earned
his apple and was designated a creative personality: students' whispers
and giggles went up and down the halls; other teachers cast envious
looks in his direction; further, the principal marked him as a possible
replacement for a retiree. The following September he became a first-year
English teacher.

Reflections.....................................

Whereas the student-teaching experience may be accurately described
as the most anxiety-producing phase of a teacher candidate, certainly
the first-year teacher would concur that this second phase is equally
neurosis-producing. [". . . *testing whether* . . ."] Consider his position:
he moves into a social milieu composed of three alien and ofttimes
hostile components—his principal, his fellow teachers, and, not the least
threatening group, his new students. He has to learn, and quickly, the
modus operandi for survival.

With his principal, he has to display his talents effectively at that
moment when and if the boss just "drops in" for an evaluative visit.
During a faculty meeting he must regulate his responses to say what
he ought to say at the proper moment and to be quiet on the right
occasion. Not too silent nor too loud nor too long.

With his fellow teachers, some younger and some older but most
of them more experienced than he, he has to establish the most reciprocal
rapport. His choices: present himself as an enthusiastic, interested
member of the profession or retreat to a pseudo-cynical, nonchalant
position.

His students in front of him force him to still another choice. He
may reveal his real interest in them, show them overtly how pleased
he is that they have come to him for counsel and guidance. Or he may
choose to maintain that "distance" he has heard some of his education
professors refer to—

Don't let them take advantage of you.

As he ponders his position in this triad, he must produce—daily, effectively and (hopefully) creatively. [*". . . struggled here . . ."*] He is most concerned about how he can turn his students on.

.... **End Reflections**

It was only natural that our CT should utilize some of his successful student-teaching procedures. He put his creatively conceived Gettysburg Address unit into action. Again the magic worked: enthusiastic kids, effective and efficient learning, creatively engendered excitement.

Then—POW! Still-insecure CT found himself summoned to that most fear-producing locale—the "downtown," or superintendent's office. [*". . . can long endure . . ."*] Classroom teachers rarely find themselves within the inner sanctum of the top man in the district. A principal's summons is fearful enough to face; but that closed, sealed envelope from the inner-inner superintendent's office with, "Would you please stop by my office after school is dismissed today? My secretary has put you down for 4 P.M.," is paralyzing.

*How did I get myself, a first-year
teacher, an innocent English major
trying to inspire junior high kids, into
this situation?*

As it turned out, in an honors English class—his pride and joy—he had the daughter of a reactionary, pamphleteering father, who might be labeled by some people as a Rightist. [*". . . our poor power to . . . detract . . ."*] Among her papers he had found a copy of THE ditto. Evidently his reaction went something like this:

*This is a sacred piece of literature
which must not be tampered with,
particularly by the editors of that
magazine. Who was the teacher
responsible for this? What radical
political party does he belong to?*

A few telephone calls—to the FBI, the school superintendent—and CT was standing before his accuser. There followed a series of time-consuming meetings with the principal, the teacher, supervisors, college professors. [*". . . will little note nor long remember . . ."*] And each day he had to face those students still as enthusiastic and committed as before. Fortunately, support rallied for CT, and all of the aforementioned professionals who had nurtured his creative spirit made his case

169

a strong one. But, and here is the crux of the story, two administrators of the upper-upper echelon insisted that he admit the guilt (or error) of judgment and apologize to his accuser. This he refused to do; and after several meetings during which he was urged "to see the light," the matter was dropped. [". . . *can never forget . . .*"]

Reflections..................................

Were there scars, a trauma? An insecurely poised CT threatened by an angry citizen who is determined to bring him to task by demanding, through his superior-superiors, an apology for a learning experience which he and his supporters thought was a creative project might be scarred, might be traumatized. [". . . *the living . . .*"] It could mean that in the future he might expect that all creativity would be suspect. [". . . *dedicated . . .*"] Perhaps, while in a creative mood, he should put blinders on his soaring visions, limit himself.

This particular citizen took issue with what he purported was a sacreligious treatment of a political eulogy. What about the other areas of literature—the relevant *Catcher in the Rye* or some lurid classics such as Shakespeare's plays? [". . . *unfinished work . . .*"] After all the admonitions of his education professors to depart from and supplement the text, he might be safer to stay with the text, a volume already given sanctimonious approval by the local school board. [". . . *so nobly advanced . . .*"] He wondered whether in all honesty, by intellectual limitations or emotional detachment, he could limit his reflection, considering only those objectives set by powers outside the classroom.

Perhaps this is only a once-told-tale. Perhaps. [". . . *take increased devotion . . .*"] But a more timid teacher, hearing about the exciting project, might be tempted to try some similar technique. After hearing the results of such an attempt, he might decide not to and continue to dispense information (sometimes referred to as education) in the old trustworthy manner: from textbook through teacher to child.

We can point a finger at the guilty administrators. We can also credit that principal and those supervisors who supported him. Nevertheless, even their efforts were not sufficient to prevent the creativity-shattering event from occurring. [". . . *last full measure . . .*"] He had to be humiliated and reminded that there was an authority in the hierarchy of public education that could bring a person to trial without defense or jury. Parents, he had been warned, were more powerful than teachers or administrators.

What happened to that lofty ideal of academic freedom which he had heard and read about so often in college? [". . . *highly resolve . . ."*] Did that privilege not extend downward to the public school classroom? A teacher's position might be easily challenged by any irate citizen and, more sadly, could be threatened by a collusion among some members of his own profession. What price, then, creativity?

.... **End Reflections**

Two years later, CT, who continued to be evaluated with high ratings for his still-enthusiastic approach to the teaching of English, left the classroom permanently [*". . . died in vain . . .*] to take a library position [*. . . shall not perish . . ."*]

Chapter 16

The Finger Job

Generalities

The dullness, the day-after-day-after-day humdrum voice, the routinized, unexciting classroom activities:

NCT
- *Open your text to page ____.*
- *Today we'll discuss chapter nine.*
- *Who wánts to read aloud?*
- *Take out your homework problems.*

NCP
- *Has excellent control over his classes. They're quiet.*
- *He's never sent one of them to this office.*
- *I vote we give him tenure.*

Kids conditioned. Administrators satisfied. Teachers collecting their paychecks. No waves. No loud voices. No upsetting of the routine.

Come in.

Sit down.

Listen.

Dismissed.

Let's try modular scheduling.
We've watched team teaching at ___ High. It's great! } CT

We want enthusiastic teachers who are concerned about kids first of all, who will motivate them to their utmost capacity.

Why don't you work with ___ next semester on that ___ unit. } CP

Enter CT, inquiring eyes searching the faces of the kids—slow, medium, fast, super-smart. Volatile, hyperkinetic, but not erratic, as his lessons proved. His passionate voice wakes them up (accepts). They are involved (share). They move (stimulate).

Get off your butt!

The former quiet atmosphere dispelled, the students have no time for dreaming. The security of the enclosing desk is gone. So is the subliminal curriculum. Involvement is the word.

Line by line, row by row they begin to quiver. Down they tumble like dominoes:

> *I'm checking out next period.*
>
> *Where'd he get that beard?*
>
> *Seems like he's turning me on, and I don't want to be.*
>
> *How'm I gonna sleep in THIS class?*
>
> *I'll scrunch down in my seat and disappear.*

Let's all take a look at each other, something besides the backs of your necks.

Nothing. No movement. They can't believe it.

Well? Are the chairs nailed down? You got glue on the seat of your pants, already?

Come on, gang. Let's try it. What can we lose? If you don't like it, we can go back to the rows.

Now. Let's just talk with each other,
not just you and me, back and forth,
at each other.

No doubt about the commitment generating enthusiasm and concern. All the passion in the voice:

You kids are great! And together we'll
make you even greater!

The demand to think:

Alternatives, people, alternatives!
There's always more than one road
over that rainbow.

The manner which turned kids on:

Swinging: *Right on, baby.*

Listening: *Tell me more.*

Bombastic: Move it!

Challenging: *Make a liar out of me.*

Gentle: *You're doing super swell. Let's*
       try it again.

Poetic: *Let Steinbeck talk to you.*
      Listen to the voice coming out
      of the pages—that Joad
      character.

Profane: *To hell with what the critics*
      say. Judge his worth for
      yourself.

The same manner which turned THEM off:

                He's more concerned about the kids'
                problems than he is about their
                grammar.

                He pushes them around intellectually.

                He's too emotional.

Two schools had selected him. Neither could contain him or his impatience with delays or administrative Peter Principling. He walked away but not without his file bulging with high ratings from subject-matter professors, from college student-teaching supervisors, from administrative evaluators. All stamped him—CT.

Where's CT?
What happened to him?
Was he fired?
Did he resign?

Unwritten. Unspoken. He just vanished.

Specifics

Bearded, liberal, divergent, he had been reared by a square brother, scion of an old, respected family:

At times, I hate his guts.
How many fathers do I have to have?

It began even as he walked through the personnel director's door:

> *Would you recommend* The Tropic of
> Cancer *to your students?*

I don't know. I haven't read it.

. . . continued as he entered the principal's office:

> *Why aren't you and your students*
> *saluting the flag?*

There isn't one in my room.

. . . approached the department chairman's desk:

> *Take down that bulletin board. It's in*
> *poor taste. Who put it up in the first*
> *place?*

My students.

> *That book's obscene.*

Which one?

> The Great Gatsby.

. . . and sat down in the counselor's crying chair:

> *Did you flip this girl off?*

No, I flipped this guy off.

Two new scenes on campus: drugs and revolt. His home was a sanctuary for the turned-on-to-trips and kids looking for a way out, exploring and deploring at the same time:

> *I've left home. My folks don't*
> *understand me.*

Parents need understanding, too.
Remember: they got you through the
first sixteen years—right?

> *Drugs are the only answer.*

Get high on life, man. Look around
you. Pills, pot, and LSD are
second-rate tickets to excitement.

He advised others who wanted to stay on the "in" but wanted change—fast. No overt action but covert assistance:

> *The principal won't listen. We're*
> *walking out!*

If your demands are worth it, write
them out—reread, rethink them—and
present them to the authorities.

They react more positively to cool
paper than to hot voices.

> *He encourages revolutionaries.*

He was unaware of the danger signals, too involved with students and subject—making them meet naturally, relevantly:

> *Why are those kids always hanging*
> *around his room before and after*
> *school?*

> *Who does he think he is—a counselor*
> *or something?*

> *My son tells me CT really reads the*
> *drug scene. He doesn't use them, does*
> *he?*

Meanwhile, back at the counselor's office, the collection of students' complaining notes:

> *CT makes us work too hard.*

> *My head hurts from thinking when I*
> *get out of his class.*

> *He doesn't kick those kids out when*
> *they use a filthy word. He just talks to*
> *them.*

and those of guilt-ridden teachers:

*I heard him say that he didn't believe
in objective exams.*

*Where does he get the time to correct
all those essays?*

*The other day he took his class for a
walk around the block to teach them
to be observant even for details.*

*No wonder that group was so restless
in my class.*

secretly, quietly piled up.
He was called to the front office and confronted with the evidence:

A brilliant teacher.

*A girl in ____'s class says you made
an obscene hand gesture in your first
period.*

Is the reporter in my class?

No, but her girlfriend corroborates it.

One of the finest minds.

*Did you allow one of your students to
read* Playboy *in your class?*

It's the only thing he'll read.

*I cannot at this time recommend not
hiring.*

Greatest respect for his intelligence.

Two weeks later:

*Why don't you resign and save
yourself embarrassment?*

He enlisted the support of his local teachers' organization, and they
filed. The hearing date was set. Nothing, nothing from the disloyal
opposition until ten days before the hearing. Then a member of the
downtown Mafia convinced CT to make a deal:

*Look. We don't want waves. You
don't want waves. We can work it
out.*

*We'll expunge your record entirely if
you leave the district.*

177

The following day his counsel, arriving at the head man's—make that headman's—office to see it in writing, was kept cooling his heels for an hour before learning how they kept their word:

The whole deal's off. See you in court.

The midnight oil flamed into a bonfire as they prepared their defense—not even time to get out subpoenas—to show cause why he should not be fired. The charges:

. . . conduct detrimental to the school and the students' welfare . . .

Reflections......................................

Many teachers, especially CT's, may be more masochistic than sadistic. The shadowy figure represented in this episode might be this kind of person underneath, enjoying sacrificing himself for others. We really don't know what any teacher is like, subliminally. But when a person makes that final decision and says to himself and the world around him,

I am going to become a committed, dedicated teacher.

he may or may not recognize the fact that a host of enemies is about to surround him.

First, in the school itself there is the student who is, of course, at the adolescent level his natural enemy, revolting against all authority, especially that represented in the grim and joyless classroom where the two meet and live together. Advertently or inadvertently it is the student who most reveres a CT, the student who carries home tales about the exciting discussions in class. Maybe only two words he mentions—sex and drugs, but they move the parent away from the boob tube to the school administrator's office to register a complaint.

Of greater importance, perhaps, is the formidable figure of an administrator. He is a tangible, nonshadowy *presence,* particularly to his teachers, who must serve or please or placate him. His potentiality as an enemy stems from the fact that his *image* as authority is as much a threat to the teacher as the teacher's image is to the student. In most secondary schools he is the invisible adversary, the man behind the closed door or separated from his teachers by possessive, sometimes officious secretaries. Part of his authority-image is the image of the absentee landlord.

Outside of the school there are the parents. They know so little of the teachers, especially at the secondary level, because they hear so

178

little about them even from their own offspring. Parents may be angry with the teacher if the student is not doing well in school and may not make it to college. At least, parents have a scapegoat on whom to blame their own inadequacies.

Also, there are the doctors and lawyers in the community, those traditional professional classes, who resent teachers' including themselves in that bailiwick. Other professionals consider teachers as gutless wonders who don't have the fighting spirit to manage their own members.

Then too, in the community at large the taxpayer always resents and envies the school teachers' long summer vacations, as well as the drain on his budget when he reads the words *school tax* on the official-looking envelope he receives each year.

There are other, personal enemies, too. Maybe the garageman down the street figures he now has the chance to give that damned English teacher his comeuppance when he brings his car in for repairs. Perhaps the TV repairman may glance at the teacher's extensive library as he installs the cable. He doesn't realize that the expense is an educational one to keep up on what's happening through the culturally oriented channels. The serviceman simply sees what he wants to see and ups his bill accordingly. Then there are the plumber, the insurance agent, the do-gooders' cookie sales . . .

With all of this pile-up in front of him, the committed CT would have to be blind not to know that he is center stage in the arena. The lions will certainly make the attempt to tear him to pieces. Yet he stays. Does he do so willingly, pleasurably?

This particularly highly creative teacher gave evidence of this kind of perspective of life when he elected to oppose those forces he knew would finally defeat him—on six counts:

Misdemeanor	*Felony*
Students	Administrators
Parents	Professionals
Taxpayers	Some colleagues

The surprise, even to him who was not deluded, was that some of his best and most loyal students gave him, wittingly and unwittingly, the finger when they stepped up to the witness stand to testify.

Is the "sign of the finger" around the public secondary school a natural phenomenon? Can the sign be given in friendship or hatred, according to the mood of the signer? Do girls understand it as well as boys? The answer to all of these questions is:

YES

Will a teacher who inadvertently, in a spirit of male humor, uses this universal language be fired, no matter what the circumstances? The answer is an irrevocable:

YES

Is the word of a highly touted, very reputable, even national-figured principal to be trusted, honored? The answer to that one, my enchanted friend, is categorically:

NO

After achieving an agreement between an administrator and a beaten-down, forced-compromised teacher who had spent hours in soul-searching, gut-tearing discussion, the negotiator said to the hypocritical, lying enforcer:

Why, you dirty sonuva bitch!

And he paid the four-hundred-dollar fine it cost him for the out-burst—smiling all the while.

.... **End Reflections**

The struggle: lawyers, arguments, exposure. Kids in the audience. Kids on the witness stand. Teachers for. Teachers against. Passionate voices on all sides:

> *He's not like any teacher I've ever
> had.*

>> *He never lets me make a statement in
>> class without giving evidence for it.*

*We never found novels and poetry
that exciting before.*

>> *I can't think that hard.*

*He doesn't give us a hard time for
cussing.*

>> *Yes, he did scare me once in a while.*

> *He should be a VP. He really
> understands us.*

I love him as a teacher and a friend.

>> *He makes us rewrite our essays ten
>> times. He never makes the dum-dums
>> do that.*

> *The radio going in the room really
> helps me concentrate.*

> *Yes, he threatened to hit me in the mouth.*

He had students who could barely read, couldn't write. They were immune to education. But his methods really blew their minds. They learned.

> *Yes, he did use four-letter words.*

He's the greatest human being I've ever known.

Judge's decision:

> *. . . one of my most difficult decisions . . .*
>
> *troubled me deeply . . . violated taboos . . . obviously some right and exciting things . . .*
>
> *. . . honest and candid . . . his own worst enemy . . .*
>
> *. . . sufficient cause exists . . . not to rehire . . .*

As he left the courtroom—and a landmark decision behind him, he was accosted by a soul brother:

Every faculty needs someone like you.

and a member of the brotherhood:

> *You're a danger to the kids, a menace in the classroom.*
>
> *We want you to stay on for a few months, finish out the term.*

Bye, bye, CT.

Chapter 17

Love Thy Students—Not!

They called *him*. He didn't have to hang on the phone to remind the personnel director who he was. He'd been on the substitute list, and evidently the school secretaries, who often are unofficially assigned the duty of evaluating school substitutes, had been impressed; some by the reports from the students themselves, others by his witty remarks as he signed in and out of the office, still others who had marriageable daughters and would "love to have him for a son-in-law." In some manner or other he had impressed, favorably and positively.

He was a reflective guy, and as he sat there in the interviewer's office, he reflected:

Do I really want to tie myself down to a regular assignment? After all, getting around to all the schools and hearing those teachers' remarks in the faculty lounges is such a ball.

Can I really face the same kids, day after day? Or am I more confident with new faces that I know I can dazzle for fifty minutes at a time?

If I were totally responsible for an accounting of my students' activities, could I stand filling out all those forms?

Am I able to keep my big mouth shut?
Asking leading questions is my forte.

I wonder how my colleagues would
accept me on a day-by-day, every day,
inquiry basis.

If they call me, do I have the upper
hand? Can I make certain
demands—and get my way? Knowing
what I do about some administrators,
can I trust them even if they verbally
accede to my requests?

Ponder, ponder. Wonder, wonder.

What the hell do I have to lose?
There's always Majorca I can flee to.

The interview was brief. They had evidently made up their minds already. He accepted.

He made one further reflection as he walked out of the office:

Those guys and gals who lost out. Do
I owe them anything? I'm really not
one of them.

Jesus Christ! They look so insecure.
So afraid. Of what? Of landing a
good job? Of just getting one? Of
doing without? Without food, clothing,
and shelter?

Reflections..

Those who hire or employ or appoint to positions—personnel directors or school principals, whichever the case may be—for the most part buy a pig in a poke. Letters of recommendation, student-teaching evaluation forms, and college transcripts are only silent evidence of an applicant's competency, while the classroom teacher is most often a talkative, noisy person, really highly dependent on his tongue for control, instruction, and response. Nothing of this latter aspect is indicated by an applicant's folder; and the oral interview, which usually accompanies the hiring process, is a verbal exchange between adults, not always transferable to kids in a secondary classroom.

There are ways in which administrators can avoid the "poke" pattern, but they rarely take the opportunity to experiment with any of them. For example, if three candidates were selected on the basis of records

183

and interviews, each could be asked to substitute in the position and classes in question with an observer present. Then when the final choice is made, on-site performance can be figured into the total assessment.

The charmer-candidate was selected by a group which had a unique indoctrination. They were adherents to a subculture that had certain unwritten criteria about their fellow members—the gray-flannel-suit image, correct prep and graduate school degrees, and the "just right" family background. He met their criteria all the way, with a plus for that charm which might have nullified all their strict standards.

Another deciding factor in this case may well have been that there were groups of students with whom other substitutes had had difficulties. With his background, this guy could handle them.

.... **End Reflections**

There he stood. There they sat. They were his, and he was theirs. Accepted and sharing now, he was faced with the process of daily classroom stimulation. Again came reflection:

As a substitute, I could hit and run.
Now *how do I keep that learning*
process going?

Each day they appear more and more
to me like prisoners of the
establishment, the institution, the
turn-off of our culture.

I wish I had them on my old family
homestead on Majorca. There'd be
plenty of activity for them there.

I must bring a sense of change and
excitement into their lives, no matter
what the risks.

Activity there was, rapport like it never happened in the textbooks he had begun to read, written by educators who had never really turned him on. Philosophy was his beat.

He picked his colleagues' brains: some responded; some resented; some ran away; some reveled in the flattery. The principal, who had been on the interviewing panel and was quite taken with him, dropped around once in a while to check on things, to see "if he could be of any assistance," he said.

Wonder if any of the other teachers,
male or female, get the same
treatment?

Only certain, well-favored ones?

Too busy to psychoanalyze, he went on his busy way. The kids began to question, which was his shining moment. He asked questions, too. The subject matter retreated into the background:

> *Can we always rap on Fridays on anything instead of Spanish?*

They rapped.

> *Can we put things on the bulletin board?*
>
> *Anything?*
>
> *Make it our own—really?*

They pinned up—anything.

The circle began to expand. What had been among him and his kids spread out to other kids.

> *Wow! You said that?*
>
> *What a groovy poster!*

The word went home on the buses and finally got into the homes themselves and into the parents' ears. Some came to school to feast their eyes and listen in on the Friday raps. Some stopped in at the principal's office on their way home.

The soon-contracting circle, the inevitable summons, and there he stood again, but not for long. He was a friendly guy, this P, a bit too admiring, but he had his official duty to perform:

> *That bulletin board with the obscene words. Uh, uh.*
>
> *Those rap sessions about world events during Spanish class. Uh, uh.*

But, but . . .

> *. . . Uh, uh.*

And he gave in. But he reflected:

What the hell kind of trap did I get myself into? The same one the kids are in?

Now I see we can't really live in the same bag.

Those parents are saying, "Don't let the outside in." "Spain only exists in

the text, not today, not with Franco,
not with the UN."

But the kids kept asking and demanding, and he couldn't quite shut them out all the way. It wasn't in his creative nature to be so easily turned off. He couldn't quite subscribe to what some parents wished to happen:

> *Let all the world—its problems,*
> *concerns, and questions—recede.*
>
> *Cut the mind off. Let it be channeled*
> *only in one subject matter direction.*
>
> *Assassinations, riots, wars—let them*
> *not enter the classroom, especially*
> *where there are children present.*

For relief from reflecting and self-doubt, he ventured into the teachers' lounge, still charming but still inquiring—and listening most of all. Too sharply his ears picked up the nuances in a discussion about the "problem." A formerly all-white school, now tokenly mixed, was to be integrated:

> *That's too bad. Used to be a good*
> *school.*
>
> *Those poor whites who have to go to*
> *that* other *school.*

And from the talking there and in those other schools at which he had substituted and listened, he came to a realization that shook him:

How can educators—teachers
concerned about kids, white, black or
whatever—allow words like "monkey"
and "black bastard" to live in their
inner thinking, much less escape to
their outer speaking?

Most temporarily employed substitute teachers or long-term subs (such as CT was designated) had probably heard the same words and wondered also. But their reflection stopped at homey discussions with their spouses. But not CT. His ire was up, his crusading spirit aroused.

He reflected—two thoughts long:

Some teachers are racist.

Someone should write a letter to the
editor.

BOOM!

186

Bells rang. Meetings were held. Principals, superintendents, professional organizers decided:

Fire him!

P softened. CT old charm was still working.

The superintendent transferred him to another school where other substitutes refused to work. Again, the grooving with the kids. But he still wrote and this time warned of pending racial tension. No one listened.

BOOM!

The riot scene. Students insisted, included in their List of Demands:

Rehire CT!

The kiss of death.

The superintendent reflected and reflected:

> 3rd Hour: *No! We'll not concede!*
> *Fire him!*
>
> 6th Hour: *More demands. And more!*
> *OK. We'll rehire him.*
>
> 9th Hour: *Riot quieted down? We'll*
> *fire him again.*

In one day three times in and three times out, the last permanently.

He drifted to a neighboring school district. After a few days the death-kiss telephone call followed.

Another district had one hundred jobs open the first day he applied. By the time the interview was concluded, the jobs had mysteriously disappeared.

Reflections......................................

They did not want nor would they have CT. Competence and inquiry were second. Conformity and silence were first. So now the classrooms in several schools which once rang with excited learning remain silent.

And so does he.

Where is he now? Up the ladder with organizations which dare to think and to inquire—sí.

Schoolrooms—no.

.... **End Reflections**

187

Part III

Every-CT: Gauged, Gouged, But Still Grooving

The lonely traveler
    And battered companions
        Stand
           Exposed;
                The all-powerful P
            Sits,
              Closed doors and secretary
           Guarding.
        En garde!
      Toe to toe,
           Eyeball to eyeball,
              Poised for fight.

              And on the sidelines—
              K   I   D S,
              Yelling for life:
              "We need you—both!

              Fight if you must,
              But for us:
              Together."

Chapter 18

CT: A Many-Personed Thing

So far presented here has been one creative teacher's odyssey, his survival against many obstacles. Also discussed were the histories of those other CT's who did not survive, who were besieged and defeated in their efforts to bring imaginative, relevant learning to their students. And as their stories unfolded, certain characteristics of their personalities and qualities of their performances seemed to emerge over and over again until an indistinct but recognizable pattern appeared to be forming.

But merely citing these cases did not necessarily delineate fully the whole multidimensional human being herein labeled creative teacher. What needs to be done now is to reiterate and materialize these repeated traits and bring them into sharper focus by means of a prototype. One figure moving through the many facets of school activities can thus demonstrate more fully and pointedly those actions and reactions that most often appear in and around most CT's.

Then, too, the one CT's story covered a span of many years. On the other hand, the experiences of several other CT's illustrated specific instances, those fateful and often fatal moments of truth. Therefore, just as the qualities will be gathered and distilled in the single exemplar, the circumstances in which he operates will also be confined to one fairly typical day at one public secondary school.

191

Catching and holding, however, as much of his elusive, diverse personality as possible in linear time and two-dimensional space is most difficult. The best solution appears to be a trisection—

first on the obvious, external level.

and then on the perceptual and experiential level—both his positive, immediate interpretations of his own actions

and his negative second thoughts concerning other's responses to his actions.

He comes into the school building early, says hello to the custodian and asks him to open the office so that he can sign in.

He picks up his mail, daily bulletin, and assorted communiques from his mail box and walks down the deserted halls to his classroom.

He gets his head together for the day ahead.

Now let's see. Nab the first kid who comes in to go get the projector. Where did I lock up the film?

Yeah, there it is. Better get the tape recorder out, too, just in case.

Hope they're all operating today.

Lay out the materials for the kids to make the new bulletin board displays.

Papers here. Notebooks there. Oops! Better check on those new texts.

Later. The textbook clerk never gets in till second period.

Well, then. Better look up what career guidance books our library has.

Much later. The librarian doesn't show up very early either. And the library clerk is too new to know.

What does that librarian do to them that they change faces every few months?

192

Students begin to drift into the halls.
The noise volume increases.

A few students trickle into the
classroom. He bids each good morning,
exchanging jokes and small talk until
the room fills with lots of bodies,
nodes of people—small ones, larger
ones—standing, sitting, moving around.

The tardy bell clangs. The nodes, the
bodies settle down.

From one group conversation—loud
talk, heads close in intense discussion.

> *How great it is to see them get with it*
> *in a hurry now.*

Light laughter from another bunch.

Silence from the farthest one, bodies
hunched over books and papers.

> *Those heavy, noisy seats! Will we ever*
> *manage a quiet room with carpeting,*
> *comfortable armchairs, floor lamps*
> *like in homes and offices?*

He sits down with a small group
discussing a new project. He is silent,
listening, eyes darting from face to
face as they argue about and reject
suggestions, finally accepting a
suitable topic.

> *The idea sounds great but it's rather*
> *nebulous. Maybe just a springboard to*
> *the research, the thinking, the*
> *activities that will lead to learning.*

> *I can't see how they'll get it on paper*
> *without my direct leadership. But I'll*
> *let them try it on their own. I have to*
> *give them enough rope to range far*
> *and wide but at the same time not let*
> *them hang themselves.*

> *They'll have to analyze, evaluate,*
> *honestly look at the reality of what*
> *they're doing.*

Some of them don't look as though they've got it. A big question mark in his eyes.

> *If only I could get to all of them at once. An education aide is what we all need, not just for those teachers in special programs.*

Wow! Daggers from him. I wonder whether he's turned off by the idea or the kid who suggested it?

Look at her bright eyes. She's got it. Wonder if she can lead them, whether they'll accept her direction.

Decisions, decisions. It's always a matter of choices, this teaching racket. Will they accept her leadership or mine better?

Ideally, they turn each other on. My business is to facilitate the interaction among them, not between them and me.

This late in the year I'll try to get them to nail it down in written form—a notebook, a brochure. They've already done panel discussions, socio-dramas, tape, film. Now they'll have to put it down in a more formal, concrete, black-on-white presentation.

> *Wanna bet the administration won't support their printing a pamphlet? I'll have to fight them to get the paper and other supplies before I can let them go ahead with the project.*

> *It kills me to let them down, to tell them that they let them down.*

> *How can they produce anything with no budget for labor—typist, printer, artist?*

> *Nobody—but nobody—will allow them to have a fund-raising drive—candy sale, car wash, slave day—to make their own expenses. That happens*

*only when the higher-ups want
something. Then they "drive" the
whole school—students, teachers,
parents—practically nuts.*

*Walnut paneling in P's office. Jazzy
football uniforms. Indoor rifle range,
ferchrissake.*

*Millions for tributes. Not one penny
for press, paper, or paints for the kids.*

*They'll have to do it themselves as
best they can.*

*Take it easy, man. Don't waste your
energy sweating the injustices. Use it
to find solutions.*

Bet the kids find one before I do.

*Hold it a minute, gang. Are you
remembering what the topic is?*

*In rapping, they've expanded the idea
too far. It's getting too big for them to
handle.*

*How can I help them limit themselves
to essentials, maybe make a
cooperative project out of it with
groups or individuals handling
different phases?*

*Bright Eyes is eager enough, but she
can't do it all by herself.*

*How can I get her to see that she
needs subgroups, a coordinating
committee to feed the information into
the big group to select and edit?*

He glances at the clock.

*The time! The goddamn time! My
worst enemy. I've got to get to the rest
of the kids.*

*Cover the curriculum! Get those books
read! Practice those skills!*

*How can I get them to do it now? I
know they'll need them someday, but
the kids can't see any sense to it now.*

195

*Sometimes I can't either. But I have
to do it—all, for each one's needs, and
interestingly.*

And with my bare hands yet.

*Well, I'd better shoulder them out of
the nest, cut the cord, let them try to
organize this into something
workable—on their own.*

*I'll be back in a few minutes to see
how you're getting along.*

He moves toward his desk.

roll book

essays   tests

hall passes   absence lists

absence cards   STUDENT   overdue book notices

requisitions   observations forms

catalogs   summonses

progress reports

He checks the roll book; initials a
dozen papers, cards, and
authorizations; adds notes here and
there.

*Good God! What does the dean of
girls want to see her about? She's
been absent for three weeks, and I
wanted a chance to rap with her
today.*

*If that witch gets to her before I do, I
may not see the girl for another three
weeks.*

I want to listen to that girl.

She only wants to talk to her.

He writes comments on and signs
progress reports.

*How I'd like to have the time and
permission to write an objective
report: "John has learned fifty new
words this month. He has learned to
write sentences with capital letters
and periods 80% of the time. He can
report orally the highlights of a group*

196

*discussion, but he does not contribute
his own ideas and opinions."*

*Whatever happened to that plan to
release the kids early for one week to
make time for parent-teacher
conferences in lieu of report cards?*

He puts a hand on the student's
shoulder and speaks a few words. The
student smiles.

*He hates the classwork. No wonder.
He's failed most of his life, according
to his cumulative record.*

*But doing this God-awful paperwork
for me makes him feel needed and
important.*

*Most of the time I can get them to feel
good about what they're doing, about
themselves.*

*Amazing how the "please's" and
"thank you's" get to them. And telling
them how well they've done even after
I've written it on their papers.*

*But I've got to get him back to where
the real action is.*

*You did a good job stamping those
book cards.*

Accentuate the positive—first.

*It sure needed doing, but will it help
you learn to read better?*

If it's negative, put it in question form.

*About time you got your nose in that
book. Otherwise I'll have to put that
book in your nose.*

*Scoldings they can handle if it's done
good-naturedly.*

*Wonder whether my department
chairman, evaluating me at this
moment, would understand. Or would
he mark me down for bruising the
boy's psyche?*

197

He moves among the silent group,
each one working on something
different: essays, workbooks, texts,
library books.

How're you getting along?

> *I can't quite tell whether it's his
> thinking, his natural pace, or some
> distraction. Boy, he's so slow!*

> *If I stop him to talk or correct his
> work, maybe I'll interrupt the process
> and he'll never get back on the track.*

> *But on the other hand, sometimes just
> an encouraging word is enough to
> keep him going. And sometimes it
> isn't. And sometimes just a pat on the
> back. And sometimes nothing at all.*

> *Somehow it all boils down to
> personality vs. personality, his traits
> rubbing against mine, hopefully
> melding.*

> *We stand toe to toe, communicate
> eyeball to eyeball.*

> *Somehow it jells—eventually. Today.
> Tomorrow. This hour. That hour.*

> *Anyhow, most of the time it does.*

> > *When it doesn't, it hurts—him and me
> > both.*

> *Well, man, what are you going to
> do—this time?*

> *I'll try letting him open to me.*

> *Hm-m-m. He isn't going to open.*

> *Move on, Mac.*

How're you doing, buddy?

> *He wants me to hold his hand, lead
> him through the work
> step-by-baby-step.*

> > *Don't get too close to them. Keep that
> > distance. Maintain respect. Don't
> > touch.*

198

*Maybe it's not so hard. Let's see if it's
like some work you've already done.*

> *He's so terrified of failing that he
> avoids all decisions. That way, he's
> not responsible if he goes wrong.*

Let's try it this way.

> *This is hard, but I've got to arrange it
> so he feels successful—by his own
> doing.*

Read the directions to yourself.

> *It's even harder to know when to
> reinforce or when to punish—which
> way will challenge him to move on.*

*Now tell me in your own words what
it says.*

> *It's hardest of all to decide the exact
> method that supports him while he is
> required to make his own choices.*

*You've got the first part right. Now
can you see any other way of doing
the next part?*

> *He hasn't quite got it. Questions,
> questions! Which is the right one?
> Which turns off? Which turns on?*

> *Over and over, a different way each
> time, till he gets it.*

*Good going! Makes you feel great to
solve it by yourself, doesn't it?*

> *Reward him this time. Follow the
> experts' words: "Reward leads to
> learning. Punishment leads to
> learning but with possible negative
> side effects."*

> *Next time—who knows?*

> *If I could only get the psychometrist
> away from his testing long enough to
> sit here and observe and then confer
> with me.*

*Now try the exercises. Be sure to
check your work over. Then compare
it with the answer book.*

I guarantee you'll have fewer errors.

He doesn't look too sure.

I'm not too sure either. I feel as
though I've hoodwinked him, even for
his own good.

A Madison Avenue manipulator in
teacher's clothing.

Careful of that gut-level thinking
there, friend.

Then let's find out why the errors.
OK?

Wow! I sure get involved with these
impossibles, dreamer that I am. One
of us has got to keep his eyes on the
goal: their change of behavior, their
learning.

What a tightrope to walk! Friendly
but not familiar. Concerned but
objective. Humanly close but clinically
distant.

He sits down in an empty chair next
to another student.

She's been staring at the same page
all period.

Well, time to get out the old probe,
jar her loose.

Not too close, baby.

Everything OK?

If I ask her to tell me what she's
read, she won't be able to.

So what do I try?

Didn't see you at the game Friday.

Boy! Am I slipping! That line is an
opener with boys only.

You've been looking kind of dreamy
lately in this class.

Can't remember what she's interested
in.

200

*But I'm expected to remember
everything about each of them every
live-long hour.*

New guy? I'm jealous.

*Watch it! Who knows what sex pot
lurks behind that distraction.*

*Say, those doodles you've made aren't
bad. Spend much time around horses?*

By George, I've got it! Horses.

*My vibes must be rusting. Got to keep
tuned in on them, their egos first.*

Mine? Well, someday.

*Have you thought about riding in
some of the parades around the
community? Might be fun.*

Grooving now.

*Maybe the library has something on
training horses.*

That she'll read about.

*Here's a pass. Let me know how you
make out or if you need help.*

Keep those channels open, baby.

He starts hesitantly toward a solitary
figure tilting back in his chair, staring
at his knees.

*Well, I can't avoid him. The sit-in
dropout. The one I can't find the
handle on.*

*Jeez! I hate to admit there are born
losers, but this guy has almost
convinced me.*

*So what do I know about him? No
success in school. No outside
activities. No girl. His family couldn't
care less. Bombs out with friends.*

I wonder if dope's got to him—yet.

*Looks like a dead end. But I've got to
keep trying. This day. This hour. This
moment.*

*No. Tomorrow I'll check his
file—again—in the counselor's office.
Maybe. Just maybe some teacher
touched him one time.*

> *If the counselors would only let us in
> on some of their secrets.*

*Once is better than never as a
starting place.*

He calls them all together.

> *Damn! Look at that time!*

*Never got back to Bright Eyes and
her group that's about to ride off in
all directions at once.*

Must do something about it.

Can I see you a minute after class?

> *And start with them tomorrow.*

> *And barely time to wrap it all up
> today.*

So what have you done? What do you
need?

> *Yeah, I could get it in a minute. But
> better they should try to locate a
> camera and film on their own first.*

>> *One thousand dollars a year it costs
>> me to stay in teaching—audiovisual
>> aids, magazine subscriptions, mileage
>> chasing after equipment, admissions
>> to special events.*

>> *What a headache trying to keep up
>> with the knowledge explosion because
>> the Board doesn't.*

The passing bell rings.

He listens and talks to some of the
kids who linger and help him pick up
books and papers.

> *Always something extra—a moment's
> time, a word of advice, sharing in the
> pleasure one of them feels in the good
> work he's done.*

202

They finally leave, and he does, too,
locking the door behind him, a rather
tricky operation with a partially
jammed lock.

> *I asked for a repairman weeks ago. If
> anything's missing I'll get it—in the
> neck.*

He moves with the milling mass.

> *My God! These swarms get bigger
> every day. No time to stop to talk or
> the logjams pile up.*

> *All it takes is one poke in the ribs to
> start a riot.*

> *Well, that's one way of
> communicating.*

*I wonder how boy meets girl around
here.*

> *What a racket! Lockers banging, feet
> pounding, girls shrieking.*

*Does the noise pollution start here, or
is this just an echo of what's out there
beyond the fence?*

He turns about face abruptly and
catches up with a young man.

*That report you promised me. Where
is it?*

> *I don't know why he's avoiding me.
> Maybe I pushed him too hard. Maybe
> not enough.*

> *I sure enough rewarded him, letting
> him do his own thing. But maybe
> there might have been a better
> payment.*

He retraces his steps, stopping a
loud-talking, hot-pantsed girl.

Why weren't you in class today?

> *She's been absent more lately, silent
> and withdrawn in class when she
> does come.*

Used to show me her poetry. Good,
too. And I told her so.

> *Could be the boyfriend? Trouble at*
> *home? A different crowd she's running*
> *with?*

I certainly told her how much she's
got going for her.

> *But she can't seem to keep the faith*
> *in herself.*

He stops by a serious-faced boy
stashing books in his locker.

Come and see me after school.

> *I've got to find him a job or he'll drop*
> *out for sure.*

> *His father's in the hospital. Cancer.*
> *His mother split. Three younger*
> *brothers.*

> *So what's your problem, buddy?*

Congratulations on your award!

> *Golly! That fruit her folks gave us*
> *was good. From their own yard. How*
> *could they spare it with their size*
> *family?*

> *Every minute of those after-school*
> *hours with her was worth it.*

> *She's slow. But what guts!*

Did you get those dittoes I sent?

> *Her students rave about her student*
> *teaching.*

> *She looks like a swinger. What great*
> *plans and materials she has—and*
> *shares.*

> *Wonder how long she can last. Will*
> *the administration turn her off, sour*
> *her, or make her more determined?*

He finally enters the teachers' lounge.

Hello, all.

> *Same old crowd. No new faces.*

*We all seem to have our self-imposed
ghettos, our R and R areas.*

*Science boils coffee on a Bunsen
burner, Home Ec on a stove.*

*No commingling during conference
periods.*

*Well, now. What should I move into
the middle of today?*

*The team teaching discussion over
there? The learning theory one? The
game coming up? Who's making it
with whom?*

Or start something new?

Change. Today, a different tack.

*Coffee first. Now just sit down and
unwind. Let the guts and grey matter
all slide out.*

*What happened today? What worked?
What bombed? Where do we go from
here?*

*Choosing, planning, trying, evaluating.
Ongoing and constant. The end of one
unit becoming the opening for the
next. Hopefully.*

*Guest speaker coming up. Film for
that bunch. Field trip. Panel. Drill.
Demonstration. Debate. Reading.
Research. Writing. Rapping. Testing.*

*All it takes is experience, skill,
imagination, time, energy, courage,
assistance.*

       Let me outa here!

He begins to listen in on the various
conversations, then joins in.

*Did you get that loan for the house,
Jack?*

       Always money problems.

*I'd like to help him out, but Marge
objects.*

Trying to stay sane and married and
teach too can be a hassle.

Think we'll beat those guys from
across town? It's about time.

      Really don't much care, but they seem
      to.

Who are you going to vote for at the
next union meeting?

      Union *is still a dirty word around*
      here.

Would you send Armand to see me?

      His PE teacher may be right, but I'd
      rather get the dope straight from him.

      If he's been copying his older
      brother's old essays, I've been had
      again.

      I figured him for real. Well, I learn
      something every day.

      I'd better.

How's the wife and baby?

      Wonder why I let myself get trapped
      in this small talk.

      It's not small talk to them.

      I hear he runs off at the mouth about
      his problems to his students, too.

      My education professors were right:
      keep your personals out of the
      classroom.

He gets up and goes to a small,
disorderly room just off the lounge.

That old ditto machine sure makes a
racket, doesn't it? Can I help?

      Wow! How come I never noticed her
      before?

      Why doesn't P introduce them at
      faculty meetings?

When it gives me trouble, I make mad
love to it. Like any woman, it usually
comes around.

Instruction from and to the gut level
whenever possible.

This your first practice teaching
assignment?

> *My worstest hours, my practice*
> *teaching days.*

Gee! I'll never forget that TT who let
me in on the trade secrets: cultivate
the powers—the secretary and the
custodian.

> *And those supervisors! Millions of*
> *them, all telling me what to do.*

I'd never have made it without those
tests and worksheets TT gave me.

Now it's my turn to pass the goodies
along.

How's it going?

> *How come I feel so comfortable with*
> *her?*

> > *I sure don't with my own ST. He's too*
> > *structured and opinionated.*

Here we are, only months apart as
colleagues.

> *How can I encourage him to go to it*
> *head-on without also warning him of*
> *the shoals and sharks ahead?*

His commitment, enthusiasm, and
idealism are sticking out all over him.

> *Does he have to learn it the hard*
> *way—what the real teaching world is*
> *like?*

How can I help him? What's the way
in?

> *If I don't warn him ahead of time,*
> *he'll get it right in the mouth from his*
> *P on his first job.*

I could say nothing.

> *Can't leave him in the dark.*

I could say it flat out.

> *And end up sounding like a smart ass, too.*

He leaves the lounge and searches out his ST's college supervisor.

I'd appreciate any help you can give me with this fellow.

> *I know he's making it with those 35 kids he has now.*

> *But can the same plans, methods, and materials work for five or six classes a day of all kinds of kids?*

He listens carefully while CTP-CS relates his observations and makes some suggestions.

> *Isn't that wild? I've been staying in the classroom to be of help.*

> *What ST really wants is for me to get out so the kids know he's in charge.*

There you go—preaching alternatives and not practicing them.

You bet. I'll bug out. Thanks.

> *Misperceptions again, baby. I can't afford them.*

> *Would you believe teaching is a dangerous occupation and may be hazardous to health? Theirs? Mine?*

He continues down the hall and stops in at the VP's office.

Hi, Bill. I hear Mario's been suspended. What's the buzz?

> *He's been doing great work for me lately.*

> *Bill's awfully hard on them.*

His math teacher is also impressed with his improvement.

> *Then, too, he never seems to take time to get all the facts. Has he asked Ken or me?*

I can't see that smoking in the head is such a crime.

208

> > *I doubt that he ever sees the large picture.*

Well, if that's the way you see it, I guess that's that.

> > *If I'd only known sooner, I might have been able to get him off with a lighter sentence.*

> > > *If I'd even opened my mouth, I might have got my head blown off.*

He hurries on to the nurse's office.

Was it the flu or a bum upper from one of the pushers in the locker room?

> > *When they say they're sick, I believe them.*

> > > *I wish I knew more about the symptoms. I can't tell the difference among the stoned, the stewed, and the sick.*

Temperature of 103°? How could he even sit up in class?

> > *Whew! My lucky day.*

Two errands done. Next stop: counselor's office.

Hank's not in? Well, can you find the material from Polytechnic? He said he'd get it for me.

> > *He's really on his game about college entrance requirements.*

> > > *But he's so unrealistic about these kids.*

> > > *Most of them have to go to work right after graduation, if not during school, too.*

> > > *They can hardly speak English, much less read it. And Hank has nothing—no information, circulars, resources—to help them with their needs.*

He leaves as the passing bell rings.

209

Do I have time after school to stop by
Poly to pick up their brochures and
films myself?

Wonder if the math department could
relate multiplication tables to gear
ratio on hot rods.

Wonder if the auto shop teacher,
whoever he is, could help.

Do we have an auto shop?

He ducks into the main office and
puts an affectionate arm around the
girl at the switchboard, the secretary's
assistant.

If it's Tuesday, this must be supplies
day.

Brighten up your life and say yes to
me. You do have an extra ream of
ditto paper.

Golly! Those kids in third period are
a great bunch.

Imagine them trying to show up the
journalism scholars by putting out
their own paper.

I've got to let John know what we're
doing. Will he or won't he see what a
turn-on it is, a chance for my group to
improve their language skills.

He's got to.

He makes his way back to his
classroom and opens the doors for his
impatient, jabbering students.

OK, gang. Let's cool it and get to
work. Even before the tardy bell, just
for a change.

Boy! It's a sweat firing them up for a
new subject area.

What topics have we eliminated so
far, the no-no's?

What is education all about anyway
if they can't rap about what interests

them most? What good is school if
they can't hash out their
problems—put into words what bugs
them—at this moment?

They were great about going along
with the limitations on three-letter
topics: God, sex, and pot.

Not word one about abortion, drugs,
cohabitation, why priests can't get
married. I remember the last teacher
who tried. Sure miss him around here.

I'd have loved to learn more about all
of them myself.

You people did a magnificent job
making that community pollution film.
Did I tell you that the Chamber of
Commerce may show it at this
month's meeting?

All right, now. A little less bragging
there. You could have done a lot more
with that notebook on capital
punishment.

So what's the hot topic right now?

I hadn't thought about bussing as a
possibility. That new transfer has
more good ideas than I've been giving
him credit for.

Are you sure you want to pursue that
subject? I can't see that you people
are suffering from the rising cost of
living.

They've brought in most of the
records, magazines, books, and other
goodies.

And they're a hell of a lot better
dressed than I am, too.

Well, the eighteen-year-old vote is
already going through the legislature.
We could check on where it is.

Wow! She's really uptight about
bussing.

*Is she worried about finding enough
boyfriends of her color-type in another
school?*

*Yes, military service would be a good
topic, but for how many of us?*

*If we research censorship, a lot of
people—parents, the librarian, P—will
be on our backs.*

*Sounds like bussing is really on your
minds. Let's get with it.*

*How do we start? Who's for bussing?
Who's against it?*

*Well, you can't all be on the same
side or we'll have no discussions, no
chance to explore the whole range of
alternatives.*

*I never expected to find so many of
them in favor of it.*

*All the letters to the editor of the
local paper have been against it. And
I've heard that the editor goes to
every board meeting just itching for a
fight.*

*What are we going to do with it when
we get all our information collected?.*

*We've already done a film, a
notebook, oral reports.*

*A panel discussion to present it to the
student body is a good idea.*

*Can we get the kids released from
classes to come?*

*We'll never be able to get the
auditorium this late in the year. Too
many athletic award assemblies
booked in.*

*Any other possible ways of presenting
it?*

*Better to keep these controversial
topics confined to this room.*

*Public exposure makes them all
quiver and shake. They worry about*

> those telephone calls from irate
> parents and blue-nosed busybodies
> even before the project is begun.

They've got to have room to explore,
but I can't let them fall off the cliff,
like with being suspended.

> I'd better not get too close to the edge
> myself or I'll be suspended,
> too—permanently.

If we're all together, maybe the way to
go is straight ahead: fact finding,
scientific inquiry. No opinions, no
editorializing, no guesses, no beliefs.

Say, how about packaging it and
sending it to Nader? If he can make
cars, food, even money safer, maybe
he can make living safer—help
decrease Chicano harassment and
alienation.

> I never cease to be amazed about how
> they always get to where it's at.

> All they need is time and the freedom
> to respond without fear of reprisal or
> ridicule.

> I sure hope the administration doesn't
> dampen their ardor, "finger" them
> again.

Are we ready to divide this into
topics, assign committees, elect
chairmen?

> It's always tremendously exciting
> when it works.

> It's tremendously enervating whether
> it works or not.

> And every time I generate enough
> enthusiasm to lift us off the ground, I
> end up feeling starved.

Just about refueling time. Let's pick
up from here tomorrow.

The passing bell for lunch rings. The
students bolt for the door, and he

213

spends a few minutes picking up the
room and debating with himself.

>Like a horse I'm starved.

>>And horse fodder is what they serve.
>>Maybe I should start brown-bagging
>>it.

>But some things I do better in the
>cafeteria.

>>Might meet some new faces in the
>>lunch-bucket brigade.

>There's the fence mending to do with
>George. I didn't get that info to him
>before the deadline.

>>Maybe I can break ground with
>>BJ about tape-recording those
>>books.

>Since Joe's going to be the summer
>school P, I want to tout him about a
>job. Now? Later?

>>Maybe I can catch up with
>>Hank. Would he chew
>>cheek-by-jowl with us slime?

>Tom wants the word about the new
>interdepartmental American Studies
>course. Do I hard sell? Drop hints?
>Push everyone's enthusiasm for it?

>>But if that student activities' director
>>is at table, he'll 'club' me again, on
>>top of student court and junior class
>>sponsorship.

>Got to find out where the guys are
>gathering for poker Friday night.

>>Today I'll go. Tomorrow—is tomorrow.

He surveys the room to be sure it is
ready for the teacher who will use it
the rest of the day. He hurries to the
cafeteria, acknowledging greetings,
smiles, and waves along the way.

He enters the noisy, packed room and
looks about as he waits in the long
line, speaking with several colleagues

214

as he had planned to do and with
some he hadn't.

Good afternoon, ladies.

> *Every time I see that flock of
> close-to-retirement biddies picking
> and talking, my blood boils. They
> have files full of tests, worksheets,
> oldies-but-goodies books that they
> share with no one.*

*I got some circulars from one of the
publishers today. Looked like good
stuff. I'll send it to you. Let me know
what you think of it.*

> *So new, and so lost, she is. Must ask
> Marge to invite her and her husband
> to dinner—soon.*

> *Sure could use some beer to wash
> down this spaghetti.*

*What's the dope from the last
meeting, Ed? Does it look like the
strike vote will pass?*

> *I hate like hell to miss anything going
> on there. I'm never sure that
> secondhand news is all the news.*

> *I'd rather ear- and eyeball it myself,
> feel the air and smell the emotion as
> it happens.*

He and his ST who joins him at
lunch, head for the shop complex.
They enter the electric shop filled
with a mob of boistrous young men.

*Settle down, fellas. We can change
the plan, like laps around the track
instead of the field trip.*

> *Sometimes it seems to take forever to
> build my kind of rapport. They know
> pretty well where and when I'll bend
> and won't bend.*

> *I wish I could be as sure when I'm
> not here, when a substitute has to
> deal with them.*

215

*The planning is tight. The kids are
usually forewarned.*

Still . . .

OK. Let's get going. You know the
route. And the rules.

*Sometimes I wonder whether the
hiatus is worth the hassle.*

planning
trip slips   lunches
liability   extra work
administrative veto   additional supervision
class coverage   colleague's envy
weather   snafus
last-minute cancellation

Not completely shaped up, they ship
out—ST in the lead with a few
students around him and he following
the group, rounding up potential
strays and moving with them into the
center of the ragged column.

*Those ST's are a godsend. Wish we
could get more of them. The boss
thinks they're a pain.*

*Bet you can't add the numbers on the
license plates as we pass.*

*Not the parked ones. That's too easy.
Try the moving ones.*

*Were there leaves on those trees last
week? How do you know?*

*See that dude? After he's passed, tell
me everything you can about how he
looks—clothes, features, height,
weight—just like cops have to do.*

*And what do you think he does for a
living? In his spare time?*

*Estimate the distance from here to
that post. Now pace it off. How close
were you?*

*How tall is that building? Anyone can
count stories. How many feet? How
tall is one story?*

*Yeah. Groovy threads. How much
would the pants, shirt, coat, and shoes
cost separately, all together?*

*How would you do math if you
didn't have fingers?*

A few blocks from school they arrive
at a construction site. They walk into
the nearly completed building.

Let's hold it here till our man comes.

*I know you want to see the whole
works. But remember, gang. We voted
to restrict ourselves to learning only
about the telephone circuitry today.*

*Maybe we can plan another trip to
see other parts of it. It's all up to you,
how you behave today.*

> *Now what made me say that?*

>> *Another trip is impossible. Got the
>> word from the head man today.*

*Simmer down now. You can't take in
the information when you're busy
putting out other news.*

*Remember last week's quiz? How
many ways can sound waves go at the
same time?*

*This is Mr. Sims. He'll be able to
answer your questions.*

The students stand and listen for a
few minutes.

>> *Hm-m-m. Their attention is beginning
>> to wander. And so are their bodies.*

> *They're getting lost in the technical
> lingo.*

>> *These PR people could use an
>> educational methods course or two.*

> *It seems so simple to me: find out
> where they are and what they're
> interested in. Then bridge the gap
> between them and the subject—fill in
> the blanks, the unknowns that they*

217

*want to learn and I know they must
learn.*

*Well, if it's going to begin, I'd better
start it.*

*I don't understand. How do you know
which wires to hitch together if you
have so many strands of the same
color?*

What do the colors mean?

*How do you learn to tell one from
another?*

*How do you remember what you
learn?*

*It's worked before. Hope it does this
time.*

*Be not-so-bright in front of them and
they're less afraid to ask questions
and risk sounding stupid.*

*He sure doesn't see what I'm trying to
do. He's so wound up in his own
thing he can't hear what the kids are
saying.*

*Maybe it's just me who doesn't get it.
Maybe they know it all already.*

*How do they learn it? Their cars?
Stereos? Ham radios even?*

*Maybe I should forego the field trip
and ask the kids to bring in their own
gear to work on and explain to the
rest of the class.*

The boys' VP unexpectedly appears.

*Good grief! What's he doing here?
Checking up on our whereabouts?*

*Did I forget to clear something with
someone?*

*Maybe he wants to find out what's
keeping them out of his office at this
hour.*

Maybe he's after one of them.

218

He moves to one side with his
superior, speaking softly and intently.

*Oh, come on, Bill. Can't it wait until
we get back? Tomorrow even?*

*He's been so eager about coming. Do
you have to take him away right in
the middle of it?*

The VP utilizes the loud approach,
mentioning the crime.

> *Sonofabitch! Has to use the kid to
> warn the rest of them.*

The man and the
trying-to-become-man leave amid
oinks and grunts from the students.

*Shove it! Right now! We all have to
follow the laws, even the ones we
don't agree with or make.*

> *I'm with them all the way.*

> *What a mess this is going to be to
> unwind.*

> *No thanks to him, I've got a whole
> new scene to work through.*

> *Still, I'm glad I'm not in his shoes.*

*Don't blow your cool, baby. Tool up.
Get them all together again. Keep
them on the orders of the day. Don't
let them replay the last scene.*

*It's about time for us to head back,
too. Let's go around by the rear
entrance and see as much of the place
as we can.*

He and his ST talk quietly with two's
and three's at a time as they funnel
their way through painters' scaffolding
and furniture being moved in.

*Does it look like the kind of work
you'd like to do? Why? Why not?*

*Do you think it takes special training?
For how long? Is it expensive?*

*Does it look dangerous? Would you
have to buy your own tools?*

What kind of future does it have?

*What would it take to get a job like
that?*

> *Reinforce. Reiterate. Expand.
> Evaluate. Over and over.*

> *Boy! I'm bushed! Never the easy way.
> Always the unexpected, no matter how
> carefully I plan.*

They arrive back on the school
grounds.

So long, gang. See you all tomorrow.

He starts for his morning classroom,
then stops suddenly.

> *Oh, no! It isn't Student Court day.*

> *It is.*

He turns and heads for the drama
room. As he enters, he finds the court
already in session, the justices sitting
around a table on the stage and the
desks on the classroom floor filled
mostly with whispering wiggling
students.

He finds a seat near the stage and
watches and listens to the proceedings
and the reactions of the spectators.

The case is against a teacher who
allegedly used profanity while
chastising a student.

> *Why does he insist on prosecuting?*

> *He's too straight to go looking for
> trouble. He never did in my classes,
> anyway.*

> *But maybe he's not so straight that he
> didn't deserve the bad-mouthing.*

> *The teacher wasn't very discreet
> either, losing his cool that way.*

220

*But I can't blame him. I've lost
control many times, even let out an
obscenity or two.*

*I must be awfully lucky that no one
finked on me.*

Some students in the audience begin
to speak out, making remarks about
kiddie-cops and prejudiced justices.

*The court hears all evidence from
those involved in the case. Those not
involved are reminded that they are
only spectators, not participants.*

*Those who wish to cheer and jeer are
excused to the athletic field, which
this courtroom is not.*

After some shouting, scuffling, and
ejections, handled competently by
several strapping boys, the case
continues.

*Wow! Am I impressed! The
prosecution's evidence is
tremendous—taped depositions and
witnesses.*

He eyes the clock.

*Damn! Where does the time go?
Marge will be furious. I'd better forget
the poker game Friday.*

*Get some tickets for the ballet instead.
Is there time? Is there money?*

Golly! Both those lawyers are sharp.

*Wish they'd show the same drive and
control in their research papers.*

*What we really need here is someone
else, a government teacher, to assist
them with procedural problems.*

Finally the case ends. As everyone
files out, he asks the court reporter
for the tape of the proceedings.

*Better get this to P before all kinds of
rumors start spreading.*

Maybe I can head off trouble by
keeping them informed.

Maybe make more trouble.

He drops off the tape and goes to his
classroom to collect his gear.

By the door a young man waits.

Oh, no! Not him again. He's got to
quit trying to make me into his father.

The boy hands him an envelope,
mumbles something, and goes off
quickly.

Almost blew it again. How did he
know it was my birthday?

He calls down the hall to the fast
disappearing figure.

Hey, man. Come around again
tomorrow. I want to hear about that
slick new car of yours.

They wave to each other. He picks up
his briefcase, a stack of books and
papers, a tape recorder and heads for
the sign-out desk and then his car.

As he pulls out of his stall, he begins
to reminisce, reflect, and mutter.

Wish I had some magic to change me
into a civilian so I can drop this
full-time involvement bit when I leave.

Try to turn the old mind off, baby.
Think about home, her, the
kids—m-m-m, a drink.

Nice to remember the smiles on my
kids' faces.

Except that one guy. He was smiling
when the VP pulled him out of the
field trip. I'll bet he's not smiling now.

Great participation on the Student
Court today. I think they've really got
it. They sure don't need me.

Can they keep it going without the
administration sniping at them, not

222

really listening to what they're
saying—and doing?

If I had to pick out the most obvious
difference between teachers and
administrators, I guess it would be
the quality—better, the skill of
listening.

I try like hell to hear everything the
kids say. Not just the words but the
feelings in the voice, the deeper
thoughts behind the words.

> *I'll bet there isn't one of those jokers*
> *in the front offices who can repeat*
> *what I say immediately after I've said*
> *it.*

But the kids seem to listen. They
respond to what I say. We listen to
each other, learn from each other.

> *What have I ever learned from*
> *administrators? Fear, for sure.*

> *Have they learned anything from me?*
> *Would they admit it if they did?*

By golly, now! That team teaching
scheme looks like it might actually get
off the ground. Not this year. Maybe
next.

Should we present it now. Firm it up
more?

An outline or a dissertation?

> *What way will grab them where they*
> *live? They must live somewhere, but*
> *sometimes I wonder.*

> *Decisions, decisions.*

> *Work, work.*

> *Teaching is plain, dirty, damn hard*
> *work.*

> *Backbreaking.*

> *Spirit shattering.*

How many hours do I spend
planning, producing, motivating,

facilitating, evaluating, trying again?
Who's counting?

> *The higher-ups always seem to get an*
> *hour or better for lunch, have time to*
> *chat with buddies, make a phone call*
> *home, even shut the door and just*
> *empty out their brains—hm-m—*
> *daydream or who knows what.*

> *The higher up they go, the lighter the*
> *load of papers they take home, the*
> *thinner the briefcase.*

> *I've never found that head counselor*
> *in his seat when the tardy bell rings.*

> *Are their names on the sign-in sheet.*
> *Do they get it if they don't sign in?*
> *Who's checking?*

Who'm I bullshitting now? I love it!
Yes, I gripe. That's a fringe benefit
grunts like me can demand—the right
to gripe.

> *Wish I could say it to them, the way*
> *I feel right now. With me, it's clear.*
> *The words are right. With them, it*
> *gets all muddled.*

I love it like a luscious mistress. It
piques and satisfies my curiosity, my
need to experiment, to be active, to be
successful, to relate to people—all
people of any age, intelligence,
background.

It happened today with the kids in
the hall, with my ST, with the office
girls, with CTP-CS.

By golly! It even happened this
morning at my bastardly
neighborhood gas station. I'm into the
mechanic for $150 for that job he did.
But next time I bet I can do it myself.
If one of my kids will let me borrow
his tools, maybe even his hands and
head.

224

*I just can't keep from being a teacher,
a learner, both at the same time, at
any time or place about anything with
anyone.*

*My job—hell, my life—is to make
personalities—unique, free, responsible,
sensitive, intelligent human beings.*

>*Well! Will you just listen to the little
>tin s.o.b. now!*

>*So all right, already. So what breed
>of cat are they, those administrators?
>What breed do they produce? What
>effect do they have on students' lives?*

>*Surely they must have some.*

*I wonder if they ever put
complimentary remarks into those
damning cum records.*

>*So what do they do for a living?*

>*Can't see a bit of artistry in what they
>do. They're just high-paid
>technicians—pencil-pushing and
>paper-shuffling hourly wage earners.*

>*Their work is not their lives, their
>wives. It's just the way they make a
>living.*

>*No involvement, no concern about
>human lives or ways or feelings.*

>*They don't care. Why should I?*

>*All we are—students and teachers—is
>the means to their jobs. They need us.*

*But face it. I need them, too—students
and teachers and—it gags
me—administrators. People are my
medium—my paint, pen, piano.*

*Sometimes I feel that I need them so
much I care more about them, the
kids and my colleagues, than I do
about me.*

*I lie! I need them for me. But not like
a bloodsucking vampire. More like—if
they don't grow, I don't.*

225

*I feel strong enough, have enough
faith in myself as a person to know I
can change, behave differently.*

*And I think I can make others feel
strong, secure, show them how to
change themselves to be whatever they
want to be.*

*I can learn about them. And I know
or can learn what to do to help them
become what they could be.*

*Sometimes I wish to hell I didn't love
them so.*

> *I know. I still sound like a little tin
> god to me.*

*Well, taking it from the top—in the
beginning was—is—those kids!*

*Boy! Do they keep me loose! Just
when I think they're going to zig, they
zag.*

*When I'm worried about how to turn
them on, ZAP! They turn themselves
on.*

> *Of course, I zig and zag, too. The
> worst times are those moments when
> I'm not quite sure whether to push
> harder for fear they'll go over the
> edge.*

> *And then, sometimes, I have to draw
> back, make them stand on their own
> feet, let them fly or crash by their own
> choices.*

*Man, when I see all those eyes bright
and shiny, I know I'm where it's at,
where they're at.*

> *But I can't sit around in euphoria
> forever. I've got to lasso those
> mavericks who split from the herd.*

*They don't have to run with the pack
all the time, just some of the time.*

*How can I help them to recognize
their individual strengths that need to*

226

be intertwined to make the group
strength?

> *Maybe their individual strengths*
> *aren't all that strong, that sure, that*
> *secure underneath their bravado*
> *facades.*

What can I do to strengthen them,
make them confident by making them
competent?

Only when they know they have
individual worth can they afford to
release some of it for the group and
not feel they're losing something—their
identity, their security.

And boy! With some of those individuals,
and even with some groups, the round-
up takes forever.

How much time and energy do I expend
on the sit-in dropouts?

Maybe I should be spending it with the
turned on, or at least with the neutrals
who can be turned on more easily.

How far can I bend over backwards before
my spine—and my ego—snap?

How far do I have to reach out,
trying to meet them a great deal
farther than half way, only to get
my hand bit off?

> *My God! What's a handsome,*
> *talented human being like me doing*
> *here in this enemy camp?*

Well, damn it! It's the truth. The only
truth I know. My truth.

I hate teaching. Oh, but I love
teaching.

All the roles—teacher and learner;
superior, colleague, subordinate;

227

accepter, sharer, stimulator;
innovator, facilitator, evaluator.

Ah, the pleasure and pain of it all.

I must be nuts. It helps.

The day rushes by like it had already
left before I got started—the dusk even
before the dawn.

Not enough help. Well, some. And
only from the kids.

Not enough energy.

Not enough time.

Sometimes just not enough me.

Chapter 19

How Was I Born?

What the hell is a handsome, talented human being like me doing in a place like this?

CT asked himself this question in the last chapter. Yet at some point in time and place he had also said to himself:

Teaching is for me. Teaching IS me.

Why, indeed, should he choose teaching as a job, a career, a lifelong way of life? There is hardly a redeeming feature to recommend it.

Socioeconomically, a teacher has no status and almost no salary. Everyone takes him for granted. Like England, there will always be a teacher. And although he must train as rigorously as those entering other professions—for instance, doctors and lawyers—nobody, including him, acclaims him by honor or wealth as a professional. He receives only begrudged compensation for the long investment of time, energy, and money he spends on his training. And even those factors which might

LOW STATUS
AND LOW
SALARY
BEGETS
NCT

229

substitute for status and salary—a sufficient number of job opportunities and the security of tenure—are presently being taken from him.

NO EGO INVOLVE- MENT BEGETS NCT

Another hazard directly concerns his ego. Like the assembly-line worker in an aircraft plant or the steno-pool typist in a large insurance company, a teacher never sees the end product. He participates in one time-place segment of students' lives. He never knows how they all come out. Subliminally, he may be more concerned with the process than the product of learning. But he feels more successful and worthwhile if, like the lawyer who wins a case or the doctor who saves a life, he can also see concrete results.

NO INTERNAL SUPPORT BEGETS NCT

Still another barrier to entering the teaching field is the teacher's symbolic role in the perception of students and parents. A teacher is harassed by each and both separately and in chorus. Secondary students view him as an omniscient, omnipotent, unbenevolent despot. He is an easy, accessible target for any and all of their aggressions and frustrations, whether they are generated by home, peers, school, or the world situation. Parents find him just as accessible for scapegoating their own inadequacies with their children. Most parents never consider that the homes they establish are the primary, most pervasive educational institutions their children ever learn in. They expect teachers to form and reform their children's attitudes, concepts, and skills. In the accountability argument, they consider neither themselves nor their children as two sides of a triangle of responsibility. They see only that the teacher must do everything and anything that parents cannot or will not do to and for their children. And if he fails, he is blamed for everyone's failures.

NO EXTERNAL SUPPORT BEGETS NCT

The general public—the mass, as different from students and parents, is too often unwilling to invest in its own betterment, as demonstrated by the almost-sure defeat of bond issues and tax overrides for the past few years. It is also unwill-

230

ing or unable to see that change is the necessary, inevitable result of the cultural process. Thus, the public sees fit to protect itself *immediately* in terms of health and safety—ABM systems, Medicare, the new pollution-control legislation. It cannot see, much less visualize, the long-range protection and social advancement that accrue from competence in thinking, expression, problem solving, discovery, and knowledge gathering. The public supports teachers neither financially nor psychologically, fearing that new, different, status-quo-upsetting ways will leave it naked and powerless.

In terms of subject matter, the teacher is cornered on two sides. In any field he is handicapped by lack of equipment and materials, the "tools" that he needs to practice his trade. Whether it be text or library books, typewriters, socket wrenches, groceries, volleyballs, paints, sheet music, test tubes, slide rules—there aren't any or enough or substitutes for the hardware he requires. As if that weren't enough, he has little choice or voice in developing the curriculum, the material to be covered in the year. Someone else has set means, goals, and standards which he must meet and match. Never mind that the silk-purse-designed subject matter doesn't match the sow's ear students. He must make them meet, fall in love, and marry till graduation do them part.

NO HARDWARE AND NEGATIVE SOFTWARE BEGETS NCT

So, then, with all these barriers and hazards indigenous to the profession, what makes a human being want to dedicate his life, give up what little fortune he may fall heir to, and forego his sacred honor to enter the teaching field? All the reasons ever given can be summed up in four words, each identifying a different relationship between the would-be teacher and the world around him: self, student, subject, and society.

In the first place, a creative teacher is well aware that the first person any human being must please in anything he does is himself. This perception is less egocentric than it appears on the

SELF-IDENTITY BEGETS CT

231

surface. His own gratification far outweighs the happiness of someone he helps. He feels no guilt, indebtedness, or envy as the other person may feel. On the other hand, if he satisfies himself to the detriment of others, then he is the one to feel the pangs of inferiority and jealousy. Thus, he chooses teaching, one way to help others and thereby please himself, as a road to self-satisfaction.

He knows himself as well as he knows anyone. His reflection in the morning mirror is clearly etched—a few shadows, perhaps, but only around the edges. Nothing blurs the core, his own ego. Happiness, success, fulfillment—all the philosophical terms spell teaching to him, with himself in the role of teacher. Whenever the outside-world lights dim and the images appear on the interior screen behind his eyes, he sees himself before, among, around students. Teaching is his real self in the world, his own interior world and the one "out there" too. He would know himself, and would have all men know him as teacher, facilitator, purveyor of ideas, stimulator of thinking, encourager of inquiry.

STUDENT STIMULATION BEGETS CT

Second in his thought is the reason for his title. To teach means someone to be taught—children, kids, pupils, students. He may say romantically, "I love 'em"; perceptibly, "I want to share with 'em"; or even insightfully, "I will facilitate their learning processes." But if he is again asked why, after first responding, "It's my life and living," he will say, "The kids turn me on," or "We turn each other on," or "It seems to be my mission in life to assist young people, or any people, to become better acquainted with the mysteries and excitements life has to offer." He wants them around him always, sometimes the more the merrier. But he also recognizes that with all his dedication there will be some of them he can never reach, that his influence will never leave a mark where he has touched them. Not pleasurable to him is the life of papers, books, and things—the lonely life. It is people and action he seeks, craves, and demands. The thought of his own group, his own kids, his "class" as it is inaccurately referred to, keeps him alive and well through the darkest moment, of which we have seen many throughout these pages. The expectations of excitement, discovery, and success with those kids gird him handsomely for all the battles.

After himself and people, and only after these, comes his desire to pursue some nonhuman activity. Somewhere, somehow, he fell in love with an author, those historical figures, that logical numerical abstraction, an expressive medium, a rational process. He wants to stay close to it, to them, forever, to delve into their most intimate and intricate parts. For this satisfaction he weds the educational system to those students whom he will enthuse to the same ends. And he will pursue graduate studies in his subject in order to become even more knowledgeable and aware, always returning to his classroom with his exciting discoveries to share them, to stimulate others to discover them. He proclaims himself to himself: I am a teacher-historian, teacher-artist, teacher-mechanic. And these are my fellow enthusiasts, my apprentice aficionados, my protégés. With them and their fire we can surmount the obstacles and climb the ignorant mountain together."

SUBJECT EXPLORATION BEGETS CT

And finally, the choice could not have been made without the sustenance that it is all worthwhile—the struggles, the hardships, the sacrifices. The world, he believes but cannot prove, is more good than evil. Progress, even in the transforming and refinement of the human spirit, has been made. Teaching is hopeful work. Change will come, however slowly. He may feel that he has failed some students during their time-place moment in his classes, but he also believes that they will be somewhere retrieved and brought to their own realization. To him, each today is better than yesterday, although not as good as tomorrow.

SOCIAL BETTERMENT BEGETS CT

233

And still the enigma persists. He chooses teaching *despite* the tribulation, not *because of* the rewards. But that answers only the why. Where, when, and how did he decide gladly to bear the cross, foolishly to believe he could leave an imprint on a world that couldn't care less what it is or where it is going? The real beginning of a CT has to have its genesis somewhere.

Before he committed himself to THAT DAY analyzed in the previous chapter, and all the days like it, there were those stimuli from hundreds of pleasurable days which moved him to his final resolution: "I want to teach." Where and when was the seed planted? How much nurturance was necessary in order that fruition occur? Did one of his CT's of the past do it in a moment? Was it the culmination of years with a CT here and a CT there? Was the choice made in an inverted process and his commitment made out of "I certainly can do it better than that!"? How did he survive the putting down, the side-swiping and the under-gutting, the SOP's of American public education, and persevere?

Or is he a mutation, a "natural," a teacher's teacher whose insights—from something in the conscious experience and unconscious perception and perhaps even his heredity—are so constructed that they culminate in an enlarged, super-insight that embraces all human conditions for all time, a creation unique—all-seeing and all-perceiving in almost every teaching instance?

These questions raise the issue of "teachers are born, not made" or "teaching is an art, not a science," which implies an emphasis on the affective rather than the cognitive aspects of teacher characteristics. But this chapter is more concerned with that initiation, that primeval instance, when his ego selects from the various experiences and/or id-constructed phenomena the alternative that moves him into the teaching role. He recognizes that this world is where he belongs. Further, he perceives that the pleasures outnumber the pains, his choice inures him against threats to his ego. His commitment shelters him from any violence to his life style. His allegiance prevents any encroachment upon his creative domain.

To begin at the beginning, a CTC (Creative Teacher Candidate) may choose sometime during his elementary education to become a teacher. If he does, his course is clear. He might be expected to become a dedicated member of the profession. And it is possible that he really does make the choice this early.

In the first place, creativity seems to be stimulated more at this level than at any other. Although he is required to sit in prescribed seats in the almost-ancient desk-behind-desk pattern, he is also allowed, with others, to regroup chairs for reading activities. His eyes are stimulated by the bright colors of photos and painting on the walls and bulletin boards. Frequently, his ears absorb music and narration which elementary teachers utilize as accepted parts of the total education process. His hands, too, are kept busy with scissors, crayons, paints, and hammers, which teachers encourage him to use. Music, art, and construction are all part of his social studies unit. Even science and math have been included in the Gestalt. His muscles move in free play, unencumbered by rules and competition.

RICH ENVIRONMENT BEGETS CT

Secondly, programs like the Progressive Education Association during the thirties, the present-day software of new insights and experiments in child development, and the hardware of technological materials and methodological know-how based on these findings have developed a syndrome of creativity among the entire corps of elementary school teachers. They seem to be more concerned with innovations. Often, classrooms are ungraded, and more open. Individualized instruction and programmed learning are very evident. More often than in secondary schools, this type of less structured, more flexible system is the result of federal and foundation funding, used to conduct experimentation connected to research. The pace is geared to the child. The environment is rich in the depth and range of learning opportunities.

INNOVATION BEGETS CT

235

Thirdly, each elementary teacher is a personality more highly motivated to consider each student as integral elements of humanity. A closer human relationship develops between the teacher in grades one through six or eight and his students with whom he lives each day, all day, in the *loco parentis* situation. In later school situations, this intimate, home-like atmosphere begins to disintegrate.

The above pattern, then, may have been the inspirational motivating climate that moved CTC toward accepting the teaching role as a life pattern. If so, he moves naturally into the rest of the programs established by the system without the tensions produced by negative experiences such as turned-off teachers, poor facilities, and nonrecognition. He conquers them all because he has come to accept himself in the teacher-image. Interestingly enough, if his choice is made at the elementary level, he usually sees himself as a teacher of children, not subjects, or of all subjects and not exclusively of one specialized area. But the future CTC may not yet have made his final decision and he moves on to the junior high school, or intermediate school, which in the thirties and forties gained prominence as an experimental, exploratory experience for youth aged eleven through fourteen. Evidently, the transformation to a student-centered curriculum, more

successfully culminated at the elementary level, has never been quite completed at this level, now labeled *secondary*. At the same moment that the inroads of Progressive Education stimulated the re-examination of the purposes of education for the teenage group and a report was made blueprinting new goals for this level, two counterforces postponed any real transformation of the secondary school.

A war called II intervened. And one of the losses—if not to the entire world, at least to that segment called secondary school, was an abandonment of any real change in the format of the

236

high school of the forties. Progressive Education stopped at the elementary level. The second force came from the colleges and universities, where pressure was exerted to squeeze the junior high school into the high school mold, which remained largely college preparatory in aim.

Thus CTC is denied the stimulus of creativity at the junior high level, which was originally designed for that purpose. He is also denied an intimate relationship with one teacher for one year and must relate to his mentors, now five or six each year, through a more impersonal association. In this new environment the subject matter looms more important. Therefore, his interests, like those of his teachers, may change from those in people to those in things—books, materials, ideas, discoveries. Possibly this may be the phase during which some creativity may be lost. One teacher out of six may be able to help him maintain the spark first developed at the elementary level. Highly motivated by one inspiring teacher, he may be able to continue his drive to become a teacher.

But considering *all* students who pass through this stage, it is extremely unlikely that any high interest and enthusiasm for school is generated at this level. Few if any students deliberate about a possible life's work in teaching during junior high school. Nor would they opt for it even after thinking about it. The falling-off of emotional involvement with school and school people begins about the seventh or eighth grade. And there are several internal and external reasons for the beginning of this disenchantment.

Externally, as already mentioned, there is the greater number of teachers he must cope with. And there are also greater numbers of everything else. His concerns are dealt with by several offices—registrar, counselor, attendance, vice-principal, health. He has to diagnose his own ailments before he knows where to go for treatment. Then, too, the size of the student body, the greater

DETOUR
BEGETS
NCT

ESTRANGEMENT
BEGETS

NONINVOLVEMENT
BEGETS
NCT

PROLIFER-
ATION
BEGETS
NCT

237

complexity of its socioeconomic and intellectual make-up, the number of buildings and the acreage they cover, the variety of activities within and outside school hours, the increased number of school hours itself—all these differences may have some bearing on CTC's past or present commitment to teaching as a career.

Another external force is the kind of teacher present in the junior high school. In the thirty years since this level of schooling was established as a separate entity, there has been little or no professional training related directly to this stage. Almost without a dissenting voice, all secondary teachers desire to teach at the senior high school level. They teach in the junior high because it may be the route to senior high, a place to start. It may be the only area in which jobs are available, and these teachers aspire to move on to higher levels as quickly as possible. If these models alone are accessible to the CTC, he stands little chance of finding a dedicated, enthusiastic exemplar whom he can emulate.

As to his own internals, these are harder to pinpoint and can be mentioned only as possible assumptions. His traumatic entrance into adulthood, a fairly reliable fact, may produce harder-to-prove results. Short or long, the period of change may usurp his drive toward any future goals. Usually, he sees everything only in terms of the present—today. He turns more inward, scrutinizing his body and soul as they are transformed even as he gazes. His relationships with peers, previously more egalitarian, now become more competitive, especially with his own sex, and more suspicious and stand-offish with the opposite sex. Thus caught up in the turmoil of his own innards, living more in a world of his own and his peers' making, he feels little influence from things and people outside of it.

With all these factors going against him, it's small wonder that he may move into the three-

NCT
BEGETS
NCT

REVOLUTION
BEGETS
NCT

or four-year high school scene engulfed in disillusionment. Or at least he may approach that senior high school, that ninth or tenth grade, a neutralized CTC who may or may not be reactivated by means of this new experience. The turning point for CTC may well be at this juncture. He now sees the process of teaching in its most realistic manifestation after his many years of day-to-day contact. It is one career he knows most fully. And according to the number of dedicated, creative teachers he meets, his enthusiasm will rise or fall. Perhaps the only continuance or genesis of his interest comes from any warm, close teacher-student relationship developed at this time.

REALITY
BEGETS
NCT

To the dampening influences evident at the lower level, now even more manifest and erosive, may be added a few others. His peer group exerts a stronger force upon him, encouraging him to stay with them and their ways, to forsake all adults, authorities, and establishments. He dare not join the Future Teachers' Club, even though he still consistently pursues his goal, for fear of the reprisal and excommunication that could result from his open commitment to establishment activities.

FEAR
BEGETS
NCT

He rebels against his teachers as representatives of all the adults against whom he holds the grudge of the generation gap. No hero now is the figure before him as he had envisioned him in elementary school. Now the image is an ogre to be overcome by various subtle harassments. The needle is even more flagrantly applied to those teachers who are more subject-oriented, who try to push their bag down their students' throats, forgetful of including students in the planning and development of the curriculum. Neglectful of the creativity of their charges, they do not often engage in nor are they encouraged to participate in diversive dialogues about the problems, large and small, that confront students in their daily encounters with their environments, local and universal.

Compounding the revised image is the students' perception of the teacher in alignment with and adjunct to the administrative forces of the school. The former ally in learning is now seen as the uncritical interpreter and enforcer of orders from GHQ. Counselors tell students to take certain courses and not others, steer them into prescribed activities and away from those that they might want to explore. And the teacher reinforces these decisions, seldom listening to his pupils' explanations and rationales for other preferences.

ALIENATION BEGETS NCT

Through this maze of forces and counterforces CTC struggles on. It is even less likely now than before that any new recruits have joined him. And so they stand on the commencement stage, the two opposed components, separating and perhaps never to be reunited in the brotherhood of learners. The CTC, the acceptor, shoulders his bag and heads for college to go through the routine that will gain him his goal. The other, the rejector, (at least for the moment), and in the majority, has had it. His diploma is his freedom warrant. Never again, he swears, will he have to associate with establishment figures and operations. He'd rather be dead than like one of *them* doing *their* things.

And so CTC enters the college scene. It may be almost free or expensive; two year or four year; community or state college, or university. And he may be joined at this point by newly initiated recruits. His fellow travelers may have arrived from the service, directly from high school, from a year or so in the workaday world, even from the dropout ranks dropping in again. There is no evidence as to why they decide at this juncture to re-enlist in the corps.

Again, CTC may have his interest, enthusiasm, and creativity heightened or stifled. For in the institutions of higher learning the instructor has moved farthest away from human or personal involvement with his students and has become more concerned with the subject that intrigues him. Simply to say, however, that the least inspired teaching is done at the college level is not necessarily to condemn it. Not all scholarly types are poor teachers. Nor are all those who put the teaching process first always as inspirational as they envision themselves to be. The syndrome is more complex. And for too long college and university administrators have not faced the reality of their professors' personal dynamics.

Among the faculties of most collegiate institutions exist two types of personalities who have elected to become a part of the academic community. The first of these historically is the scholar who finds the climate and resources of collegiate institutions necessary and conducive to his research. He desires only a cubicle in a library or a computer or lab facilities. His employer, however, insists that for this privilege he pay the price of teaching. So for part of his time he stands before small or large groups of students hating every minute stolen from his real love—research. When CTC faces this personality in the classroom, he may react in one of two ways. He may move so far away from his goal of teaching that he never returns to complete his training. Or he may be more determined than ever to recreate a more perfect image.

THING-
ORIENTATION
BEGETS
NCT

Fortunately, enough of the other type, the dedicated college professor, is operating to maintain an inspiring atmosphere in some classrooms. These CTPs' main purpose is to arouse creativity, curiosity, and enthusiasm in their students. An encounter between this type and CTC can impel the latter to complete his own training in order to perpetuate the same inspiration. There is no doubt that during this phase of his undergraduate education, CTC is influenced considerably by professors who play the role he aspires to. And so CTC arrives at his B.A. degree, having followed his possible dream to this point. And as he takes leave of his former work, he also leaves former classmates—fellow sufferers in lecture halls, labs, and seminar circles. They go on to professions, businesses, government services, or to pursue advanced degrees.

CTP
BEGETS
CT

He begins his more intensive professional training in education—philosophy of, history of, psychology and sociology of, methods of, materials of—those studies that will relate him to the educational system theoretically and practically. He

ALLIES
BEGET
CT

and his now-more-experienced fellow travelers soon become aware of new faces. Some he has never seen before. Some are vaguely familiar. And some are decidedly familiar, perhaps even one of those outspoken, turner-downer separatists from the establishment who has opted for a return to the fold as a means of getting to where he can rearrange the fences.

LIKES
AND
UNLIKES
BEGETS
CT

For the first time in his long journey toward his now-almost-touchable star he finds himself surrounded by only those who are pursuing teaching, albeit at different levels, in different subject areas, even from different viewpoints, as a career. And he becomes aware at this time and place of the diversity and breadth of the educational field and the human beings who people it. Many facets of these multicharacterized personalities are hewn on the firing line of the graduate school experience. Yet other capacities are the results of varied backgrounds, skills, and learnings, in earlier school and non-school circumstances. And the more recent additions to this highly specialized scene have been directed there by a number of impetuses.

CHANGE
BEGETS
CT

One new recruit may be somewhat older—a person who has tried the sales field for example, and has decided that teaching, a similar operation to selling, would be a more satisfying way to live. He begins to retool his skills.

CHALLENGE
BEGETS
CT

Sometimes the newcomer may be a considerably older person, male or female, who has made a career of the armed services or family rearing and has decided that life is not finished. The financial and personal security he or she has attained now makes it possible for each to develop or refurbish those capabilities that either have been used in some other activity or have lain dormant for some years.

CTP
BEGETS
CT

Again, the neophyte may have had no desire at all to enter the teaching profession during his college career. Suddenly he has been stimulated

242

by an enthusiastic professor or has been turned on by some subject area in which he should like to continue through teaching it to younger, adolescent students.

Occasionally, a new arrival may have come to the end of his degree program with no other goal in mind but that of personal growth and enjoyment. This is particularly true in music, drama, art, or even literary or historical fields. He finds that the economics of his world demand that he earn his living—at what? Well, teaching. This type of personality is often referred to as having backed into teaching. The inference is that he is very often a frustrated writer or historian or artist or musician. Since he can't *do* it, he *teaches* it. Perhaps.

NECESSITY
BEGETS
CT

At the onset of his training CTC, along with his now fully committed cohorts, must undergo processes of examination—both self-screening and screening by his professors. He must substantiate his commitment. He and his advisors must determine whether he has the skills required to function in the classroom—good health, ability to communicate in speech and writing, adequate verbal and quantitative reasoning, competence in his subject field. Whatever is missing must be learned. Whatever is already there must be enlarged and strengthened. He is tested formally and informally by objective and subjective instruments.

SCRUTINY
BEGETS
CT

He is further tested in his classroom work by a teacher of teachers—maybe strong and maybe weak—but nevertheless ostensibly even more committed than his students to the furtherance of effective teaching. The charge most frequently heard about education professors, however, is that they haven't been in a public school classroom for twenty years and therefore don't know the territory. Be that as it may, CTC is exposed to a variety of experiences that help him to determine whether or not he has embarked on the right

EXPERIENCE
BEGETS
CT

PERSEVERANCE
BEGETS
CT

trip. He has continuous opportunities to take second and even third looks at the teaching process and his part in it.

At the finish line of his odyssey comes the moment of truth: student teaching. He is assigned to one class in a public school where he assumes all of the responsibilities any teacher has without being legally in charge. He is confronted by a variety of people—students, teachers, administrators, parents, specialists, supervisors—and a multitude of circumstances—preparation, teaching, evaluation, assisting, observing, attending seminars, interviewing. These situations are as realistic as possible.

Yet even at this eleventh hour after the years, the build-ups, the put-downs, the decisions, the worries, the work—he may even at this moment walk away from the whole scene.

Maybe a handsome, talented human being like me should be someplace else.

Chapter 20

P: A Former— Personed Thing

The Adm-image: clean-cut visage. Often athletic. "One of the boys." Not unattractive to women. Not too verbal yet communicative on his hierarchal level. Usually in control of emotions. A person who can hold his liquor, never succumbing to pagan abandonment. Rather stiff on the dance floor but willing to make the effort. Not quite nattily dressed and somewhat conservative with colors. Smoothly shaven. Strong of jaw. Not easily given to laughter. Stinting with broad smiles. Appearing to be mulling over ideas even when there are none. Often a golfer or fisherman. Rarely given to flambouyancy. Organized within himself. Always presenting a calm front in emergencies. A follower of the pre-scribed routine.

This is the Picasso-like sketch of P, the antagonist in the conflict over creativity in the classroom. A former teacher himself, he somewhere, somehow changes attitudes and purposes and directions, arriving in that exalted front office too far removed from the protagonist, the CT.

In practice, not all teachers go into a classroom determined to spend the rest of their professional lives in the same environment doing the same thing. Sometimes the change is in level, up from junior high to senior high to junior college. Sometimes it is toward a department chairmanship or special areas such as student government, stagecraft, or publications. Then again, it may be toward an intermediate level between classroom and administration—counseling, supervision, or professional organizations. In general, however, as wholly or maybe only as partially dedicated to the fight as his fellow teachers, CT nevertheless abandons his commitment to instruction and accepts the enchainment of administration.

The differences in directions depend on different aspirations. Most CT's expand and deepen their dedication to students and students' interests. Would-be administrators however, tend more to move away from those activities directly concerned with the instructional program and with people and turn almost willingly to administrivia. The differences in attitudes and purposes, precursors to direction changes, tend to be based on individual teachers' personal, social, and economic needs.

To date, no principal comes into the administrative scene at the management level. He starts in the classroom and then prepares for the principalship through certification as a school administrator. And the P-role demands certain functions which often negate or reverse those activities that spark creativity in the classroom. In the first place, CT-P spreads his caring, sharing, and stimulating thinner to cover teachers, students, all the school personnel. Then, too, he can no longer nurture his colleagues as he once did his kids because they are different kinds of people by reason of experience—or lack of it. Also, he no longer receives direct, honest feedback from either kids or colleagues. Now it is filtered through assistants, aides, and others who give him information second-hand.

The P-role itself, however, is not the only determiner of the kind of person and personality which fills it. There appear to be several types of teachers who for various reasons choose directly or indirectly to design the role to fit themselves. The four candidates are CT's led out of, driven out of, marking time in, and unfit for the classroom.

At least in the first few years, CT cannot go beyond certain fixed salary increments. If he were to receive a real living wage, he might stay committed and devoted to a career of classroom teaching. But once he feels the economic pinch and is forced to moonlight—teaching in evening schools, a part-time job in industry or as a service station or liquor store attendant, he begins to consider the administrative alternative. He may love his kids, his subject, be content in teaching. But he is led out of the classroom because he is unable to afford the luxury of choice.

Most teachers' beginning salaries are around $8,000 and top salaries may go as high as $16,000. It may take three to twelve years to get from one end of the pay scale to the other. Generally, at any level the pay differential between teaching and principaling is about $9,000.

(Incidentally, while these going prices for teachers are common knowledge, the salary ranges of untenured administrators are rarely found in print.) A reflecting, projecting CT may suddenly wake up to the fact that he cannot go on subsidizing the kids he loves in the classroom by denying those kids he loves at home.

Perhaps with qualms, he chooses the foster home of the principal's office over his real home, the classroom, rationalizing that he can effect more innovation over a broader range and eventually help more students from a principal's position of more extensive influence. So he abandons his wide-ranging advanced education—the arts *and* the sciences—and concentrates on getting an administrative credential.

On the other hand, in his concern for the larger secondary scene, he may be led out of his classroom by wandering into his first graduate course in school administration. He wants to understand such outside-the-classroom forces as counseling processes and school law. He seeks a new perspective. He desires professional growth. His professor of school administration may become aware of his potential as a possible recruit for the administrative cosmos. Seduced into pursuing another course or two, CT may find himself so far along the road to the front office that he can't turn back. His professor further ensnares him by suggesting that if he is really concerned about instruction, creative teaching, and upgrading the profession, his going into administration is one way of making it come about.

Economically or persuasively led out of the classroom, CT in some instances becomes noncreative himself, joins forces with people and things that thwart the creativity that once he stimulated and shared with colleagues and now denies. He abdicates because of role perceptions—responsibilities and limitations. That mysterious infection, fulfilling the demands of the role, somehow permeates his creative nature and sucks out his innovative vitals to leave him creativeless. Thus, our candidate number one, CT-led-out-of, joins the ranks of the accused.

If he is the CT he's supposed to be, it is unlikely that the kids, with all their problems and promises, can force him to leave his first love—teaching. Other forces within the secondary syndrome may drive him from the classroom. Constrictions and harassments can come from a frightened, rigid administration beset by various pressures—integrate or else, for instance. An uninvolved or antagonistic community may beset him and leave him unprotected by his superiors, or ignore him out of lack of information about his problems. Then again, there may be an ossified department chairman who neither encourages nor allows anyone to implement innovation. Such nonsupportive, unrewarding

247

situations can make any teacher think again about his commitment. If he doesn't leave the classroom, he may leave his mind.

As a result he may become a less-than-full-power CT and find out after a few years that the classroom goings-on—the numbers of kids, the pressures of integration, the orders from above, are destroying his own creative powers. The students do not sit open-mouthed and sparkly-eyed, hanging on his every pearl of wisdom. They challenge him on his home ground. They dare him to arouse their interest in what may sometimes be his first love—his subject, knowing that *they* should be his first love. They seek to pursue their own interests regardless of the course content. They demand. They refuse. They turn off if he doesn't meet their needs, isn't relevant.

He comes to believe that he can't reach students, that they are unresponsive, irresponsible, unreconstructable. His disenchantment, usually gradual, is erosive and debilitating. He feels that he can't teach kids his subject because they can't or won't listen and work. And he may further wonder what good it would do to pursue advanced study in his subject field if no one is buying his goods. So what else is there for him? There may not be opportunities for his line of study outside of the educational world. He may not have the courage or stamina to pursue an advanced degree and move to the collegiate empire. Therefore he must seek another road, another role within the secondary school world. The only one that drives him farthest from his frustration is an administrative one. Thus, our second candidate, CT-driven-out-of, enters the ranks of the accused.

A CT who is administration-bent may have his sights on a principal's post and simply marks time in the classroom. Not particularly involved or adept in his academic training, he sees instruction as an incidental step on the road to the front office. But he also realizes that he must serve a teaching apprenticeship first, a requirement of many state credentialing agencies to ensure a full realization of the teacher function. He may be moderately effective in the classroom, getting in a few creative licks here and there. But he is not deeply concerned with classroom dynamics and often bypasses many opportunities to implement and carry on creative learning.

He perceives the administrator's role as an authoritarian position occupied by one man not interrelated with others in the school scene. The examples he has observed have pointed the way to P for powerful. It may have been a coach who made it to the top, someone he admired at one time. Perhaps he comes from a family full of teachers and school

248

administrators who direct his efforts to the top. Or a close buddy may advise and help him find his way down the hall from the pine desk to the mahogany one. He certainly is aware of the power structures within the school where he teaches, the "ins" and "outs," and learns how others advance in it. Or he wants an easier row to hoe than instructing 40,000 students per year (200 daily-different individuals times five days per week times forty weeks = 40,000 students) and fulfills his apprenticeship only long enough and hard enough to be eligible for promotion. And another candidate, albeit a half-ass one, and this time labeled marking-time-in, becomes an accused.

Perhaps our last candidate never was a CT but only a P in CT's clothing, an NCT (noncreative teacher) that somehow sifted through a hole in all the sieves of training and backed into teaching. Unfit for the classroom, he hates those forty pairs of eyes looking up at him each day of his classroom life. The teacher next door is not his brother, his equal; but he does prefer him to kids. Still in the gang stage, he and his on-site friends chat about sports, cars, travel—anything but the education scene. But his interest in them is merely a casual one. He doesn't really care. He shares not—ideas, materials, or aid. He stimulates neither himself nor others to be curious, to discover, to pursue anything. Excitement does not exist in the classroom either for him or his students. His eyes and ears are on that goal ahead, not on the kids and subject of the day. He flees the constant close interaction with human beings that teaching is all about.

And he perceives his colleagues as he perceives himself: not as fellow travelers but as teaching dropouts, competitors in the flight from the classroom and also competitors in the fight for the well-upholstered chair in the front office. He does not see himself in the role of a facilitator of learning in the classroom and cooperator with his colleagues in building a general learning-ful environment in the total school. Rather, he seeks only the principal's office as the source of power over people, at least those people who out of free choice, economic pressure, or law are there.

NCT-unfit-for ought never to have entered the classroom at all but, as in many other professions, is there—waiting only for the escape hatch to open. Unfortunately, the route away from the classroom too often leads to the Peter-principled principal's palace.

And so he runs madly away from those eyes, that imprisoning classroom to the haven behind the gold-lettered glass door, away from the sights and sounds of kids. And thus, candidate number four, CT-unfit-for becomes an accused.

These are the reasons, in general, why teachers forsake the classroom for the principal's office. And from any of these groups any one of the accused may have come. But not all teachers in all subject matter areas move in equal numbers from the grimy green box to the paneled, carpeted one. There are some common factors of teacher and principal personality and role that have caused any one teacher to forget easily his first commitment—students' welfare and the instructional program.

All teachers are communicators, leaders, facilitators of learning—in different degrees about different things. All must seek advice, consent, and aid of the principal. All must produce successful programs. The directors of plays and concerts, the entrepreneurs of art and science fairs, the overseers of day-care training or trade apprenticeships, the sponsors of forensics and fencing are but a few. But they are unknown by all but a few people in the school or community. They are rarely sought out by administrators for even a cup of coffee. Their activities attract a minimal number of participants and generally are not cross-departmental in nature. They receive few or no funds, publicity, released time, compensation, interest, or reward.

A closer examination of the functions of the largest percentage of those who make it to the front office, the male gym teachers and coaches, reveals certain characteristics that appear to make them more available for the administrator's role than any other teachers and, at the same time, less able to generate and maintain a creative learning atmosphere for students and teachers.

To begin with, a coach performs his duties usually set far apart from the rest of the school's operations, the school gymnasium. He rarely moves out of this isolated, self-contained atmosphere to inter-relate with teachers in other subject areas. He understands little of the classroom teachers' functions and they even less of his. He deals with matter rather than mind and heart, brawn more than brain and beauty. His sphere of influence is authoritarian, regimented, success-oriented, and male rather than democratic, free, exploratory, and coeducational. Certainly there are two different worlds here, neither of which communicates with, perhaps even cares about, shares with, or stimulates the other.

Above all, coaches perceive themselves as leaders, captains of the team, in complete command of the ship. They feel they must play this role in order to unify their students' energies and loyalties to the sport—to winning. More, they are widely known in their leadership roles because through a coach's classes pass all the male students in the school. Therefore, fathers of these kids, especially those on the school team, come to know PE teachers' names and identify them quickly as they talk with their progeny about the athletic events in the school. And

250

as these dads sit in the bleachers watching the football or basketball games, they see the coach operating with his craft: he moves team members in and out, sends in orders and plays, is most visible and visibly in charge. Fathers know what his job is, see him performing it, and become confident of his abilities. There is never any question as to whether a coach today, a principal tomorrow will be able to maintain order and handle discipline problems. Every player on the team or participant in a PE program has heard or felt only too frequently the SWAT of the paddle in some coach's office.

The coach relates well to administrators. They read about him in the sports columns, know him personally, meet him after games, talk with him as he arranges for trips around or out of town. The principal seeks him out for predictions about the coming games. They meet at the local service club, where one or both have been asked to speak. Thus, the principal is more aware and understanding of the coach's problems. And certainly in the convivial, nonthreatening atmosphere of the locker room or the bar, with communication flowing freely in both directions, the coach becomes more familiar with the responsibilities, tasks, and benefits of administrators. He has a realistic model to assist him in determining his own goals, whether or not to pursue the administrative route and accept the pattern for himself.

And as they wine and dine together, at a luncheon downtown, after the principal arranges for coverage of the coach's classes, the coach becomes more closely acquainted with the businessmen and the fathers who sit in the bleachers or sponsor booster clubs. One of them may even sit on the school board. And that same one may indicate that the new school, which will be ready in a year and a half, will need a new principal, an aggressive captain like the one who runs a ship tight enough to bring victory and honor to the community, especially one who has prepared to answer opportunity's knock by pursuing or already possessing an administrative credential.

The coach's activities and role, more than any other staff member's, receive reinforcement and encouragement from both his superiors and the influential men of the community. They may have been participants in the athletic programs themselves; they may have sons in them now. The present vicarious involvement added to the recollections generate potent forces in favor of the professional advancement of coaches over all other school personnel.

So, the uncreativity label assigned to the P has been derived from a variety of sources: that former CT now led-out-of/driven-out-of/ marking-time-in, as well as corrupted by the perceived role of the model NCP; the NCT-unfit-for who stumbled into teaching and will never

251

be categorized as CT by birth or nurture but is easily accepted into the administrative ranks; that epitome of nonexcellence, the coach, whose facets and angles most nearly match the present assumed P role (or did he create it?). There he is: Mr. non-America—dictatorial, single-edged, entrenched in an unassailable office from which no creative spirit emanates to begin or continue whatever creativity remains in various classrooms. It is a cyclic process in which noncreativity feeds on non-creativity to the final disembowlment of students and teachers. And once the noncreative atmosphere prevails in a secondary school, it will persist to stultify and suffocate those germs of creativity that have had their genesis in our CT.

The portrait, then, of P is complete—as complete as it is possible to paint of any complicated human personality. He stands now, our NCP, one choice of four candidates, looming large and threatening before the classroom CT's, whose fingers point and label him—accused!

Chapter 21

J'accuse

Dear P.:

In the hierarchy of the educational
institution you stand in a pivotal
position, a communication/action
channel among administrators,
teachers, students, and the public.

YOU HAVE NOT DONE YOUR
JOB because

You communicate out of the many
sides of your mouth: Out of one side
with administrators, who are your
superiors

*We don't have any racial problems in
this school.*

*Our teachers are happy here. We
have very few requests for transfers.*

Out of another side—with the parents,
who are your employers

*Well, I had an appointment with the
faculty grievance committee, but I'll
cancel it. I'd be delighted to speak at
your luncheon.*

*I'm always glad to hear from parents
about their children's problems. And*

253

*I'll set that teacher straight, you may
be sure. Thanks for calling me.*

—and out of the third side with your
teachers, who are by your perception
your subordinates

*Why should I tell them the "whys" of
budget cuts? They wouldn't get it
anyway.*

*I can't let them know I have
reservations about making bussing
work. The law is the law, and they'll
have to follow it.*

*Teachers have no idea what
administrating is all about. They
can't see beyond their kids.*

YOU HAVE NOT DONE YOUR
JOB because

You fight for the things YOU want:

*We can't decrease class size. We have
to pack more in. How else do I pay
for the three new administrative
assistants?*

*Reading teachers! First, the extra
staff, then the machines. Now visits to
other schools—on school time with my
staff covering their classes? Forget it!*

You fight for the things your
superiors want:

*After five years of college you should
be able to keep accurate attendance
records. The downtown office is giving
me hell.*

*Don't worry, boss. All my teachers
will be at work—picket line or not.*

—and sometimes you fight for the
things your assistants (VP's,
counselors, registrars, deans,
department chairmen, managers, aides,
etc.) want:

254

> *Yes, teachers* should *discipline their own kids. That's not in your job description.*

> *Oh? Administrative credential now? Sure, you can leave early. Only don't spread it around.*

—and sometimes you fight for the
things the parents want:

> *I agree. That novel does sound kind of risque. I'll talk to the English department chairman. I'm sure they'll drop it from the supplementary reading list.*

> *I'll answer for our band instructor. Of course, they'll play for your fair. We're always eager to cooperate.*

—BUT you never fight for the things
your students want:

> *Who wants students sitting in at a faculty meeting?*

> *So, you're interested in ecology. And so are the neighbors around here. Get rid of that junk. Collect those cans and bottles and papers around your homes.*

—nor fight for the things your
teachers need to do their work:

Staff—

> *The downtown office says no more counselors. And that's that.*

> *Teacher aides? Get their parents to help—for free.*

Equipment—

> *That textbook has been good enough all these years; it's good enough now.*

> *I broke my back getting those floodlights for the field. They belong to PE, not the drama department.*

255

Change—

> *If you social studies and English
> teachers can't see eye to eye, why
> should I fight with the downtown
> office to get your team teaching
> project approved?*

> *Wait till modular scheduling catches
> on. Then we'll try it here—in summer
> school—maybe.*

YOU HAVE NOT DONE YOUR
JOB because

You use your office as an authority
over all things, all underlings:

Authority over students—

> *Stop thinking for yourselves.*

> *There will be no long hair and beards
> on this campus.*

Authority over individual teachers—

> *You must cut those lines out of the
> play.*

> *I refuse to allow you to use Catcher in
> the Rye in your class.*

> *The board won't go along with your
> plan for independent study.*

Authority over teachers as an entire
faculty—

> *The secretary will not issue your pay
> warrants until she receives your
> attendance records.*

> *You'll lose more fringe benefits if you
> push for raises.*

—and you use your office as a
stepping stone to higher positions.

> *Let's not have those hippie union
> organizers around here. We take care
> of our own.*

> *Can't make your TGIF. Our
> administrators group has something
> going that night.*

> *I can't wait to get out of here and into a downtown office.*

As well as an action/communication channel, your pivotal position is one of leadership.

> YOU HAVE NOT DONE YOUR JOB because
>
>> You are not a leader. You flinch from making important decisions
>>
>>> *I can't approve this core course without the district curriculum committee's approval.*
>>>
>>> *Let's wait and see which way the wind is blowing about parent advisory groups. We've got the PTA and boosters' club now. It's enough.*
>>
>> —or change your decisions
>>
>>> *No one in the halls for any reason.*
>>>
>>> *Send troublemakers to the office.*
>>
>> —daily.
>>
>>> *You may excuse anyone with a ticket for the game.*
>>>
>>> *Handle your own discipline problems.*
>>
>> You make only negative judgments of students:
>>
>>> *You know better than to go anywhere without your parents' signatures on these trip slips. This is the end of your service club, girls.*
>>
>> —and only negative judgments of teachers
>>
>>> *You'll have to give up this open classroom nonsense. It's too noisy.*
>>>
>>> *After what you said to me last year about no democracy in this school, I'm not about to approve your new course outline.*
>>
>> —and what is more you fail to reward them.

257

*Why should I thank him personally
for getting out that creative writing
book? He's getting paid for it.*

*Can't make the fine arts banquet. It's
my bowling night.*

Fundamental to the leadership role is
an understanding of human
interactions.

YOU HAVE NOT DONE YOUR
JOB because

You do not facilitate human
relationships.

In the school you do not set forth
clearly where teachers and students
can go to get the help they need.

*I can't release my staff to orient new
teachers. Let them find out what's
what from the veterans.*

*How many times do I have to put it
in the bulletin? Don't they listen?
Can't they read?*

You do not make sure that there are
comfortable places and the time for
everyone to meet informally outside
the classroom.

*I wouldn't be caught dead in the
teachers' lounge. Where is it, anyway?*

*They're here to work, not to sit
around drinking coffee and gossiping.*

You appoint assistants to whom
others cannot relate.

*I'm not about to submit three names
to any faculty committee. I'll pick my
own assistant principal.*

*Sure, the VP roughs up the boys once
in a while. Someone's got to show
them who's boss.*

In the wider leadership range you
misrepresent subordinates to
superiors:

258

> *My teachers will go along with this
> new teacher evaluation form. I'll see
> to it.*

You misrepresent superiors to
subordinates:

> *I'll be using this new evaluation form
> on you starting Monday morning. The
> board insists on it.*

You misrepresent teachers and
students to the parents:

> *We can't teach your youngsters if
> they're not in school.*

You misrepresent the parents to
teachers and students.

> *We can't teach youngsters if they
> come to school sick.*

And when things go wrong, you blame
others for your mistakes:

Superiors—

> *It's not my fault that the downtown
> office didn't send those ethnic surveys
> out on time. You will just have to stay
> after school to finish them.*

Teachers—

> *It's not my fault that the ethnic
> survey didn't get in to the urban
> public affairs coordinator on time.
> What can you expect from a whole
> school full of first-year teachers?*

Parents—

> *It's not my fault your kid got busted.
> Who gives him the money for drugs in
> the first place?*

Any and all listeners.

> *It's not my fault kids are so rebellious
> today—stealing, vandalizing, playing
> hookey. I'm not their Big Daddy, you
> know.*

You yourself do not relate in all ways
to everyone:

259

You listen but do not hear:

> *What do you mean, the kid's hyperkinetic? Just tell him to sit down and shut up.*

> *A fashion show? Parading around on the stage? What does that have to do with clothing?*

You look but do not see:

> *Isn't it beautiful? Not a soul on the grounds or in the halls.*

> *That new suspension rule really works. Puts the fear of God in them. Respect for law and order.*

You demonstrate no third ear and third eye—intuition:

> *I don't understand why she started crying. All I said was that she had to keep those kids quiet or else.*

> *I only know what he tells me. What he's thinking or the words he's not saying are for the psychiatrist's couch.*

You do not recognize or sympathize with the myriad problems that beset teachers and students:

> *I used to have 50 students in my study hall and they never made a sound.*

> *So what if he's a new teacher. He's lucky to have a job.*

You are concerned only with your staff's professional lives:

> *Why should I spend an extra ten minutes supervising that maelstrom at lunchtime. They can have those baby showers on their own time.*

> *How do you expect me to know he's all shook up over his divorce? I didn't even know he was married.*

You do not exhibit enthusiasm, a positive attitude:

> *Another faculty meeting. What'll I talk about?*

How many years do I have to go to retirement?

According to all policies and mandates, your primary responsibility is to see that all your students learn.

YOU DO NOT DO YOUR JOB
because

You ignore experiments and research:

I don't care what psychologists say. They don't run schools.

We don't have a budget for supplemental texts, so why release teachers to rate them on—what did you call it—a readability index? Never heard of it.

You accept too readily and without question the limitation set by high authorities:

We must follow board policy regarding suspensions, even if he did say he was sorry and wants to come back.

You can't use those films without curriculum committee approval.

You do not support your teachers and students in their innovative projects:

You'll have to call off that art exhibit. The librarian doesn't want those monstrosities cluttering up her room.

I just spent $500 to send the team out of town. I don't have $50 left to get your kids to the symphony concert.

I don't care if rap sessions are motivating. There will be no controversial discussions while I'm principal.

I have enough trouble censoring the school paper. And I won't allow any radical opinions put into print, no matter how much it helps them to read and write.

261

*The market manager complained
about one of your kids, so let's not
have any more neighborhood walks.*

*Petition or no, we will not release the
youngsters early for parent-teacher
conferences. We tried it once and it
didn't work.*

You do not encourage your teachers
and students to try innovative
projects:

Team teaching? It's not worth it.

*These goddam wave makers! Why
can't they just have the kids answer
the questions at the end of the
chapter?*

When you walked out of the
classroom and into the front office,
you picked up papers

*How can I get around to see a
hundred teachers and still get the
budget written up?*

*If the students have a legitimate
grievance, tell them to write it out
and present it when I have time.*

You put down people, teachers and
kids—

*I haven't time to visit classrooms.
And why should I? I get what I want
to know from my grapevine.*

*Can't see you today. Principals'
meeting. I'll be at the downtown office
all day. See your counselor.*

—forever.

*What's on your mind? Make it fast.
I'm very busy.*

If anyone calls, I'm out.

Accusingly,

C.T.

262

Chapter 22

OK, Smart Ass, You Do It

The only way to do it is to do it. Put my money where my mouth is. Be constructive. Put up or shut up. Try to institute change. Spend time in HIS chair, P's office.

Could I do it? Would it be possible to maintain a creative climate in a secondary school with what I know now? In the house that I might build with the only set of blocks available, would CT's, kids, and administrators be happy?

Today I take over P's job in Anyplace High School, (an urban one with approximately 2,000 students and 75 teachers) determined to be the kind of administrator who encourages teachers to utilize their creativity. How do I proceed?

My feeling is that the proper atmosphere is the most crucial ingredient for the creative act. I want to provide the right climate for all of us to work in. So first of all I must set my own domain in order: My office. Then I must "sense" what the prevailing atmosphere is, literally: watch, reconnoiter. Next I must listen closely to all of the residents of my house—students, teachers, the community. Then I must reflect, try to get at the reality of what I have seen and heard. After that I must dialogue, discuss with all of them their points of view and those that have resulted from my reflection. Finally, I must involve myself in some kind of action based on those reflections.

In order to make it apparent to everyone that I want a creative climate, I must indicate to them all that I am willing to put forth considerable effort to obtain it, just as I expect them to work at their particular tasks. I achieve this by personally experiencing the stages of creative evolution both in order to understand its dynamics and to demonstrate its workings to those who will eventually use the same techniques.

I begin at the beginning, that part of the secondary school building which is the first and last place a teacher enters each day to sign in and sign out: the main office. Here, if any place in the educational structure, rests the spirit, the totem, the all-pervasive tone that sustains or denies creativity. How can I make certain that this office helps the classroom teacher begin the day with hope, positivism, and creativeness?

Open it up, man!

Of all the three doors that lead into my newly acquired office, one is always open to the secretary. A second one remains open also into the adjoining VP's or counselor's office. But that one leading into the area where teachers, students, and community enter is too often closed.

Early in the morning all my doors are open. I am visible. I meet and greet, ask after health and family, compliment and joke with the earlybirds, the right-on-timers and the last-minuters. They realize at once that the storekeeper is really minding the store. Their puzzlements and frustrations they can express at once so that I can deal with them personally and promptly. With this positive approach a CT goes to work already primed to face that first period class creatively. It's as though part of me goes into each classroom with each of them each day. My openness and visibility, followed by my willingness to respond to him and his problem, establish the fact that as their leader I choose to put their concerns first on my daily agenda. In this way I make them aware that my primary allegiance and trust is with them, not my superiors, fellow principals, or even other staff members.

But if I am attentive to one CT's conversation at a moment when we are all firing up for the day's work, I cannot be as attentive to other teachers as they sign in for the day. A nod, a wink, or a wave does not substitute well for "Good morning, Ed." "How are you today, Esther?" My secretary, knowing my philosophies and procedures, slips unobtrusively into my shoes and continues welcoming, listening, and helping the incoming crew. As intelligent and adept at her skills as my teachers are at theirs, she is not resentful of their greater educational background nor is she bent on keeping me isolated from them. "Can he see you later today?" "Would you two like coffee in his office during

264

the break?" is her extension of my method to sustain the proper climate.

After the routine of opening the school is set in motion, I grab a quick cup of coffee in the lounge, cafeteria, or wherever most teachers congregate, perhaps catching up or continuing with some of those I missed or met in the office. Then off to walk the corridors, up and down the stairs, in and out of classrooms, around the grounds. I let the sounds permeate my conscious and if possible my unconscious now administratively centered soul.

I am aware that certain sounds relay certain atmospheres. For instance, the sound of my auto's engine comforts or disquiets me. In school, there is the quiet room where the silence is oppressive and supressive. Someone has put the lid on, and I am fairly certain that the creative process is not generated in a superimposed silence. At the other end of the audiometer is a dissonance indicating disorder, a raucousness that conveys anarchy and the riot-like sound track of *Blackboard Jungle* or *Up the Down Staircase*. The third level of sound is mixed. I hear a humming most of all, activity with a purpose and occasionally an above-the-hum noise, an argument or an enthusiastic response. And I ask:

What is the sound of my school? Why
does it sound like this? How can I
generate that sound here that reflects
a creative climate, a happy place with
happy faces—CT's, kids', and MINE?

After determining the overall sound level, I begin to listen specifically. To whom first? The students. I stand in the hash lines, eat with them in the quad, or invite them to share my table in their, the students' cafeteria. I avoid choosing those students designated by my predecessor as "leaders." Instead, I select students at random to sit with or invite them to join me. And so I listen without interrupting, only suggesting at times that they limit their conversation to talking about our school. I take mental notes.

Only after moving and listening, generally and specifically, do I at last return to my office after the school day is over and instruct my secretary not to interrupt me except in an extreme emergency; a student threatening to jump from the auditorium roof.

When I am alone in my office I recite those thoughts collected on my wanderings into a tape recorder. Then I reflect about what I heard and saw and comment into the same cassette about them. And I dictate and muse and replay, remember and interpret and play it again until there is nothing left to recall and react to.

265

Reflection in school surroundings is an important phase of my developing a creative atmosphere. The sights and sounds of school are more vivid when I am thinking about them there than when I am driving home, pulling weeds in my garden, or shaving in the morning. Even in the comparative privacy of my office, the spirit is still visible and audible. It is a difficult thing to do—reflect—in the maelstrom of a State's culture in which it has been decided that do, do, do is a more likely reality than think, think, think before doing. Maybe it's the smell as well as the sights and sounds of school that permeate my thinking about it and its pulse beat.

Not only do I collect student reactions, I ask teachers to listen also to students' reactions to various areas of school life—to write them out, tape them, but at least gather as many responses as possible about students' perceptions of our school. These I retire with into my reflecting pool, looking at them upside down, standing my brains and feelings on their heads to see them right side up.

Then I continue my specific listening by using the same techniques with the teacher set. I eat with them, chat with them in their lounge, encourage social gatherings at school, home, or bar. I listen to them in the classrooms. I hear about our school and all its works and pomps from them and return again to my office to record and reflect.

I listen also to parents—at PTA meetings, at coffee klatches, mornings and evenings. What do their children say about the school, their teachers? What do they themselves feel and think about our school? Then back to the recording board. I listen. I reflect. I talk. I listen again. I make written notes. The voices I hear in the flesh—students, teachers and parents—now are more objective sounds against which I can pit my own railings or agreeing "Uh-huh's."

And after the recurring listen-reflect stage the pieces of the next phase, Operation Discussion, are gathered and fitted into place. First a discussion with students, then teachers, then parents—a direct confrontation in which the interplay of ideas, theirs and mine, is woven into the main threads of listening and reflecting.

Out of these face-to-face meetings come more ideas; and then the retreat into reflection again follows, this time with the purpose of perhaps issuing some policy statements.

After dialoguing and reflecting I make some movements. Secondary school students and faculty members are impatient, resting gingerly on their go-go-around. I force the moment of truth and make some announcements. I can move comfortably into this area because I am confident that the preceding phases have made their imprint and that the general atmosphere of creativity has generated feelings that are

266

understanding and thoughts that are understood. We have accepted, shared, and stimulated each other—students, teachers, and parents. We trust each other.

Now comes the involvement, immersing myself in the implementation of judgment of my directives begins. But the channels through which this action flows are of a unique making. I discard the hierarchy of dissemination from the top through associates, VP's, or counselors because I feel that administrative creativity must flow directly from principal to teacher sans intermediaries. Therefore, my school's executive administration is composed of me together with a committee of classroom teachers, not departmental chairmen—teachers rotated yearly who shall for this purpose be freed of two classes instead of one for conferences. Part of their time is devoted to a direct consideration, actualization, and evaluation of the total school program. Under our directives the remainder of the staff will proceed.

I maintain my participation. I keep in touch. The fewer hours I spend in my office or off the school grounds, the greater the possibility for my releasing the creative efforts of teachers. I continue moving through the halls, speaking to anyone and inquiring about personal or school affairs. I duck into a classroom, sit down, and follow along with the instructional program. I ask myself, how's the learning going? CT has a chair in an unobtrusive part of the room where I can sit, watch, listen, take notes. Or I can move up and down the rows, around the tables asking the kids what's happening, how they are, what I can do to help them. Sometimes I'm even invited to teach a lesson.

And as I move in and out of the classrooms, up and down halls, I think about how I would have acted if I had been the principal in the stories of the undone CT's of Part Two. Having observed the many aspects of different CT personalities, I know as much of the whole man as anyone because I have seen many of his creative acts relevant to learning.

I nurture their creative efforts, especially those of first year teachers, scheduling their classes to include no more than two grade levels and no more than one low track group.

[*Remember?*
"The Screwing?"]

> *The veterans have to take their share*
> *of the tougher classes. New teachers*
> *need time to learn, too.*

I provide a sounding board.

[*Remember?*
"The Screwing?"]

> *I'm passing this sheet around so that*
> *you can gripe—about anything. No*
> *names, please. We'll rap about them*
> *all.*

I spend one period of one day each
week in their classrooms.

[*Remember?*
"The Screwing?"]

> *You plan lessons to show what you're*
> *trying to do and how you're going to*
> *do it. I want to help you implement*
> *those plans.*

With all teachers, I protect and
defend their right to create—from a
selected few

[*Remember?*
"Gettysburg?"]

> *But Mr. Supt., if you are determined*
> *to fire him because of one parent's*
> *complaint about his presentation of*
> *the* Gettysburg Address, *I insist you*
> *listen to what you are condemning*
> *before making your decision.*

—or the community at large

[*Remember?*
"Bugged Again?"]

> *We both knew what risks we were*
> *taking when you volunteered for the*
> *job of making sex education an*
> *integral part of the curriculum. We*
> *both lost. Sorry!*

—or from himself

[*Remember?*
"Finger Job?"]

> *Sounds like the kid deserved it, and*
> *the rest of the class understands. But*
> *we both know there may be*

268

repercussions. I'm with you all the
way. Thanks for alerting me so I'm
not caught unaware.

—or from the unenlightened
administration

[*Remember?*
"Creativity
and . . . ?"]

> *Hm-m-m. We do have only deficiency*
> *notices, don't we? I'll get the print*
> *shop to make complimentary notices*
> *based upon your model.*

I support and encourage them in their
instructional risk-taking—in the
classroom

[*Remember?*
"Love Thy . . . ?"]

> *It's an eye-catching bulletin board*
> *your kids have produced. Quite a few*
> *profanities and even obscenities. But*
> *I'm not sure what your purpose is.*
> *How does this develop critical*
> *thinking?*

[*Remember?*
"Bearding . . . ?"]

> *Rap sessions are a terrific motivator.*
> *But be sure what you're motivating*
> *for. Is it just to air personal concerns,*
> *like long hair or a closed campus? Or*
> *do you intend to evaluate or plan*
> *course content?*

—with one foot out of the classroom

> *I'd really like to go on your trip to the*
> *courts. Let me call Judge ____. We*
> *went to school together, and I know*
> *he'll make it a worthwhile experience.*

—with both feet out of the classroom

> *I hear we're chaperoning the noon*
> *dance, Carol. Will you teach me the*
> *new dance the kids are doing?*

269

—even clear off campus

> *I'd be honored to judge the debate.*
> *Oh, no! My wife and I are going on*
> *the Ecology Club's camping trip that*
> *weekend. Can you postpone your*
> *doings for a week?*

—and occasionally with my foot in my
mouth

> *Are you going to shave that beard off?*
>
> > *Gee Whiz! Do I have to? After*
> > *nursing it along all summer?*
>
> *OK, then. I'll grow one, too.*

At the end of the day back to the office I go—my office, your office—to
review, regenerate, that old reflective feeling:

> *Do I really ACCEPT each of my*
> *teachers, my creativity recognizing*
> *creative bits of those individuals, and*
> *attempt to maintain and foster a*
> *program that will free them to act*
> *innovatively?*
>
> > *I have ACCEPTED my teachers as*
> > *individuals and realize that as*
> > *human beings they are fallible but*
> > *redeemable in many instances*
> > *wherein blame and unjust criticism*
> > *may be the wrong approach.*
>
> *Do I share ideas as well as problems*
> *with my teachers so that the best*
> *possible solutions can be reached?*
>
> > *I SHARE my feelings, my thoughts, my*
> > *hopes and doubts with them, as well*
> > *as with my peers and superiors.*
>
> *Do I give top priority to STIMULATING*
> *the instructional program and expend*
> *the majority of my time and energy to*
> *sustain top-notch learning?*
>
> > *I move throughout the instructional*
> > *domain constantly—approving,*
> > *encouraging, and rewarding*
> > *individual and collective efforts.*

*Do I make decisions courageously,
even though they're arrived at slowly
and sometimes tortuously?*

> *I have made choices based on
> experience, training, and reflection
> from among alternatives—not always
> popular ones but amenable to
> substantiation.*

Do I demonstrate leadership?

> *I have followed or pioneered the
> paths I would have my teachers take
> so that I know the territory and they
> have a model.*

*Do I initiate and maintain a creative
atmosphere to inspire creativity in
others?*

> *I have set the scene by demonstrating
> in my own domain, showing all the
> teachers those techniques which
> engender and develop a creative
> climate.*

These things I can do and will them into being by thought, choice, and action. But there are other things I have less control over than the atmosphere and operations of the school itself. However, to these I also give my commitment and work for and include them in my periodic examination of possible activities:

> *I pressure the superintendent and the
> board to reduce class size.*

> *I protest against the many downtown
> meetings which remove me from the
> instructional scene* during class hours.

> *I demand more hardware for my
> teachers so that they can function at
> the peak of effectiveness and
> efficiency.*

> *I fight for my teachers' right to
> experiment and even to risk failure in
> the attempt.*

So, buddy mine, as I leave—our—office, what plans, practices, or essences can I leave behind to illustrate or persuade or challenge you to be what you can be?

271

1. Trust thyself, to thine own creativity be true.
2. Recognize the limitlessness of creativity.
3. Open that door—let the creativity in.
4. Listen and watch more often.
5. Make decisions only after you've heard from everyone: teachers, students, parents.
6. Build the creative atmosphere and let the details fall where they may.
7. Attend to those many-personed things.
8. Defend them against all enemies—to the death.
9. Risk something some of the time and trust and encourage your teachers to follow your example.
10. Ask yourself daily, hourly: Is learning going on here, in *our* house?
11. Will it—and it will happen.

We have run the gamut, you and I. We have been through the mill. There stands our CT, protagonist, slayer of dragons, and tilter at windmills. He did slay and he did tilt and carries with him the scars and bruises of claw and vane, our Odysseus. But his colleagues, those many-personed images, lie prostrate, undone by both dragon and windmill and lost forever no matter how creative they appeared to those students whose love they earned.

We both know now the value of that creativity that moves teachers to heroic efforts and the tragedies left by its absence. And although I accused you because you deserted me too often, we cannot remain enemies forever. A student is waiting, and only if you and I stand together accepting each other's creative natures, willing to share with and stimulate each other and that waiting student beside us, shall the windmills and dragons be bested and slain again and again until only the clear air of truth and the good earth of learning remain for his inheritance.